Into the Fray

INTO THE FRAY

THE EITELJORG FELLOWSHIP FOR NATIVE AMERICAN FINE ART, 2005

Edited by James H. Nottage

Eiteljorg Museum of American Indians and Western Art
Indianapolis

in association with
University of Washington Press
Seattle and London

ISBN 0-295-98577-1
Library of Congress Control
Number: 2005933977

University of Washington Press
PO Box 50096
Seattle, Washington 98145-5096
United States of America
www.washington.edu/uwpress

Eiteljorg Museum of American
Indians and Western Art
500 W. Washington Street
Indianapolis, Indiana 46204
United States of America
317.636.9378
www.eiteljorg.org

Editorial services and project
management by Suzanne G. Fox,
Red Bird Publishing, Inc.,
Bozeman, Montana
Graphic design by Carol Beehler,
Bethesda, Maryland
Proofreading by Patricia Bardon
Cadigan, Tucker Ink,
Tucson, Arizona
Printed in Canada

All numbers at the beginnings of
captions refer to the checklist; see
pages 124–128.

Front cover: John Hoover, *Blue
Footed Boobies* (31)
Frontispiece: James Lavadour,
Bridge (54, detail)
Details at right, top to bottom:
John Hoover, *Loon Man Soul
Catcher* (10); Harry Fonesca,
Autumn Sonata #30 (45);
James Lavadour, *Deep Moon* (57);
C. Maxx Stevens, *Book Ends: Red
Portrait* (65); Tanis Maria S'eiltin,
Resisting Acts of Distillation (68);
and Marie K. Watt, *Braid* (79)
Back cover illustration: Tanis
Maria S'eiltin, *Resisting Acts of
Distillation* (68, detail)

Eiteljorg Museum
of American Indians and Western Art

LILLY
ENDOWMENT
· I N C ·

Contents

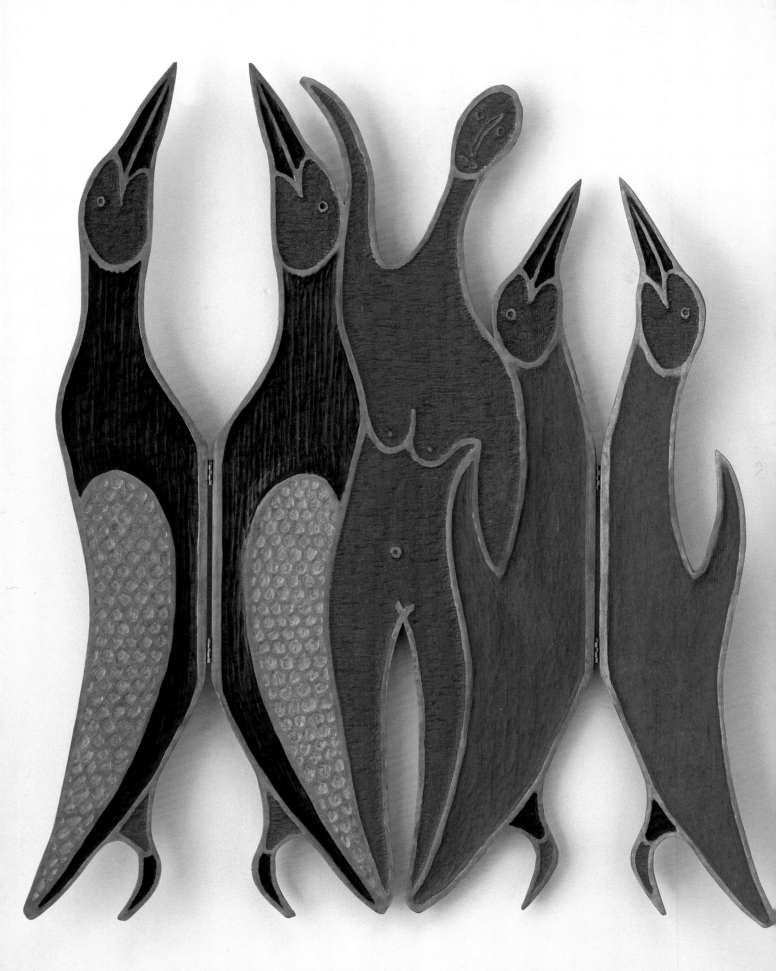

Foreword

The Eiteljorg Fellowship for Native American Fine Art is designed to identify, reward, and showcase outstanding Native Americans and First Nations artists from the United States and Canada. The Eiteljorg Fellowship is a comprehensive program intended to further awareness and appreciation of Native American contemporary art and all its diverse forms: painting, sculpture, mixed media, and installations. Each biennium, the museum awards $120,000 in fellowship prizes. In addition to the cash awards, the Fellowship project features a major exhibition of selective works by each fellow, and an important publication of their work with essays by leading authorities in the field. The Eiteljorg acquires a significant number of pieces from each exhibition for its permanent collection. A national campaign to promote these artists and their work, and the field of contemporary indigenous art in general, is undertaken to help encourage broader appreciation.

In addition to awarding fellowships to five outstanding artists, each biennium the Eiteljorg Fellowship project recognizes the lifetime achievements of a distinguished master artist. This biennium, that artist is John Hoover. Well known for his wood carvings and sculptures that explore his Aleut culture, Hoover conveys fascinating images, especially in wood. He has written, "[W]ood has always been important to me. The agelessness and beauty of wood, the many different varieties, smells, and, of course, the varied densities which make each wood a different challenge to carve and sculpt."

Now in its fourth iteration, the 2005 Eiteljorg Fellowship shows the program fully matured. This biennium's line-up of artists is a spectacular and diverse group. The format has proven successful. The Eiteljorg Museum is proud to be a part of a growing movement to recognize indigenous contemporary art.

The title "Fellowship" was deliberately chosen to characterize the coming together of artists, scholars, curators, writers, and collectors to explore and celebrate this expression of culture and individual ideas. Not only has the Eiteljorg built one of the most important collections of this kind of art, but also it has assembled a fellowship of people with similar interests. With this year's project, the Eiteljorg has brought together a cumulative total of twenty-four ground-breaking artists, dozens of scholars and writers, and a growing community of collectors and opinion makers into a circle of friendship.

I would like to thank all of those who help make the Eiteljorg Fellowship possible, but especially the Lilly Endowment. Lilly Endowment's support for the project has been fundamental to its success. I also want to acknowledge and thank Jennifer Complo McNutt, the Museum's curator of contemporary art, for her vision and unbounded enthusiasm for this art and the artists, along with Vice President and Chief Curatorial Officer, James H. Nottage, for his leadership. We are all proud of our progress so far and look forward to continuing the momentum into the future.

JOHN VANAUSDALL
President and CEO
The Eiteljorg Museum of American Indians and Western Art

23. John Hoover, *Loon Lady*, 1994. Cedar

Introduction

JAMES H. NOTTAGE
Vice President and Chief Curatorial Officer
Eiteljorg Museum of American Indians
and Western Art

The Eiteljorg Fellowship for Native American Fine Art brings together dynamic and passionate people. From museum staff and supporters to the selectors who designate the honorees, these people are devoted to creating forums for the presentation and better understanding of Native American art tied both to culture and tradition and to the larger world of art and visual expression.

The outcome is not just this catalogue, but also includes a dynamic exhibition, a challenging symposium, and a growing and prestigious museum collection. Together these results help create better public understanding of Native people and their participation in a modern world of art, which often expects them to be primitive and perhaps quaint, or even irrelevant. To achieve high ambitions for the program, however, requires more than a bit of labor.

Imagine four individuals sitting at a long table, facing screens lit by slide projections, films, and PowerPoint presentations. The discussions of the art are animated, thoughtful, and often passionate. These people are always serious, but sometimes humor breaks the tension. For hours on end, they view and review images, read artist's statements, and examine exhibition catalogues. From more than sixty nominations, they finally select a distinguished artist and five others as fellows in the 2005 Eiteljorg Fellowship for Native American Fine Art.

The designated artists receive awards of $20,000 each, the museum purchases examples of their work, and an exhibition and catalogue are produced. Who were the selectors for the 2005 program?

Entrance to the Stan and Sandra Hurt Gallery, Eiteljorg Museum, June 2005

Why should they make decisions that might dramatically affect the lives of the artists?

Patterson Sims, director of the Montclair Museum in Montclair, New Jersey, was one. He has also been an advocate for contemporary art at The Museum of Modern Art, the Seattle Art Museum, the Whitney Museum, and the O.K. Harris Gallery in the SoHo arts district. Patterson was joined by art critic Amei Wallach, a frequent commentator on art for television and radio worldwide. Wallach has written extensively on art, art exhibitions, and the art scene. Her writings have included book-length assessments of Ilya Kabakov, Joseph Raphael, and Jasper Johns, and her essays have appeared in major newspapers and magazines throughout the country. Margaret Archuleta (Pueblo/Hispanic) also sat at the table. A singular driving force in the recognition of Native American Fine Art, she currently serves as the Arts and Humanities Project Specialist for the lifelong learning center at the Institute of American Indian Arts (IAIA), Santa Fe, where she earlier served as director of the IAIA Museum. She was been a visiting professor at Dartmouth College, and for many years was Curator of Fine Art at the Heard Museum in Phoenix. Her knowledge of Native American fine art and its creators is expansive. Through publications and exhibitions, she has done as much as anyone to create awareness of the field. Finally, Rick Bartow (Wiyot/Mad River Band) provided an artist's viewpoint during the selection process. A recipient of one of the 2001 Fellowship awards, Bartow has been through much of what other Native artists have experienced.

9

Works by Fellowship artists Shelly Niro, Truman Lowe, and Nora Noranjo Morse as featured in the new Stan and Sandra Hurt Gallery, June 2005.

His success is evident through his participation in exhibitions throughout the United States, Canada, and in Germany, Japan, and New Zealand. His work is found in collections internationally.

What were the impressions of the selectors when they completed their work in 2004? Their comments afterward had a clear ring to them. Patterson Sims noted that the artists "resonate because they are very fresh." Rick Bartow felt that that he had seen an "incredible array of artists, both known and unknown, and some surprises." Margaret Archuleta celebrated a "very good group of artists that are pushing, but they are tied to who they are as individuals and as artists." Amei Wallach enthusiastically noted that "the quality of the artists we selected is so high that they deserve to be part of the international circuit of contemporary art."

As it happens, 2005 is a pivotal year for Native American artists, and not just those selected in this process. It is not just that the Fellowship exhibition opens in November. Other exhibitions are found at the Smithsonian's new National Museum of the American Indian, where one of the opening featured shows, *Native Modernism: The Art of George Morrison and Allan Houser,* focuses upon two former distinguished artists in the Eiteljorg program. At their New York City facility, NMAI has also showcased contemporary Native artists in the series *Continuum: Twelve Artists.* Nine of the featured artists are current or former Fellows. Elsewhere in the world, at private galleries and at museums, Native American Artists are receiving due attention.

The year 2005 is pivotal as well for the Eiteljorg Museum. In June, the new Mel and Joan Perleman wing was opened to the public, effectively doubling the size of the museum. A full-blown education center with studios, a library, and a resource center better serve the needs of students and adults alike. A café provides nourishment for visitors. Nourishment of another kind is featured in the new Gund Gallery of Western Art and the refurbished Art of the American West Gallery.

In light of the Fellowship program, however, the most telling addition is the completion of the Betsey Harvey Gallery and the Stan and Sandra Hurt Gallery, both of which feature contemporary art. Together they provide us with the first permanent facility in which to showcase contemporary art, including that acquired through the Fellowship program. The Harvey Gallery gives context to contemporary art of the West with powerful works by many artists, including now deceased Native painters Fritz Scholder and T.C. Cannon. The Hurt Gallery loudly places an exclamation point on contemporary Western and Native art. Visitors enter through doorways in a wall covered with graffiti surmounted by painted skateboard decks by Apache artist Douglas Miles. The words above exclaim, "Art Can't Hurt You," and beyond, vibrant art provides strong confirmation that neither the West nor its contemporary art can hide any longer from the startlingly diverse art of Latino, African-American, Asian, and Native American artists. Within this context, much of the space is filled with brilliant works created by artists honored in the Fellowship program. The great collection resulting from this initiative now has a permanent home.

In 2007, the Eiteljorg Fellowship for Native American Fine Art will complete the first ten years of the program. In that and years to follow, there are many emerging and experienced artists who will be in the fray. Yes, we know that some have wondered why certain prominent Native American fine artists have not been recognized in this program. Many of them will have an opportunity in later rounds. So, get involved. Become acquainted with the 2005 Fellows. Understand that Native culture is an essential part of Native contemporary art. Appreciate that the goal is not necessarily to make Native fine art a part of the mainstream of the larger world of fine art, but to be part of the struggle for self expression and to participate in the continually evolving worldwide definition of what art is. Understand the insight of Patterson Sims when he says, "I don't think there is a mainstream. There are lots of streams and I think this is one of the streams and it is a very important one."

When you contemplate the Fellowship artists and their work, try to anticipate the Eiteljorg Museum's expectations for future fellows. Note artist Rick Bartow's words. As a selector for the 2005 fellowship, he summed up the real goal. "We've seen what was and what is, but we are looking for what's coming."

Get Out of the Middle of the Road!

As curator of contemporary art at the Eiteljorg Museum, I find myself more alert and excited each time the opportunity arises to jump into the fray. At the Eiteljorg, we work to provide a wider audience and greater appreciation of Native American cultures, including their contemporary fine art expressions. In particular, we are able to confront notions commonly held by the public, art historians, critics, and curators about Native people and the classifications assigned to their art. Challenging old ideas is elating and terrifying at the same time. Incorporating mainstream colleagues into our process and watching them jump into the fray is so intellectually exhilarating that it gives an overwhelming feeling of hope, that the way people think can be changed to be inclusive and broad-minded.

Native American fine artists display a unique intellectual courage and conviction as they redefine and defend values and traditions that exist outside the mainstream. It is a tough endeavor, especially if their traditions frequently point out inequities and injustices that were and continue to be imposed by dominant or mainstream thinking. Using the framework or structure understood by the mainstream culture, to hang new words and ideas on a familiar grid, that is operating from the fray. A museum in the fray takes risks. Native American fine artists in the fray assume a challenging responsibility. Whether their artwork redefines the canon of beauty or presents a poignant social/political reality, indigenous artists greet the adversarial as opportunity for change, inclusion, and articulation.

As a museum, we provide a venue for the indigenous expressions whose traditions reveal so much about values, perceptions, and practices today. It is by comparison that differences in thinking clarify what is considered mainstream and what is considered the fray. Through the process of comparing, there exists the opening to question mainstream ideas and the opportunity for Native American fine artists to contribute to revelations about contemporary society based on their rich historical background and varied contemporary experiences. This mix of realities creates work that holds a kind of mystique, with elements that place it simultaneously in and outside the mainstream.

Each artist in this exhibition brings to their work a unique history, knowledge, and sensitivity beyond the formal and even the radical formats that contemporary artists engage to shock, surprise, and illustrate the contemporary world, with its sublime beauty and frightening atrocities. There is a lot to be learned from the aesthetics and knowledge Native American artists employ in their interpretations. As artists and audiences gather and wrestle with the issues of art and representation, it becomes clear that the further into the fray one investigates, the more complex and challenging the dialogue and debate. There are many perspectives even within Native cultures, not to mention differences influenced by media and mainstream thinking. Even so, we still believe that working from the fray and pushing on the middle gets Native American artists closer to fair and accurate representation and well deserved recognition.

66. C. Maxx Stevens, *Book Ends: Shunatona Dance Steps*, 2004. Book, mixed media

It is remarkable to be in the position of standing behind Native American fine artists with a view of the world as it transforms into a place where their voices are acknowledged for great insights and contributions to both their own and mainstream or popular cultures. So jump in, because the middle of the road is the last place you want to be.

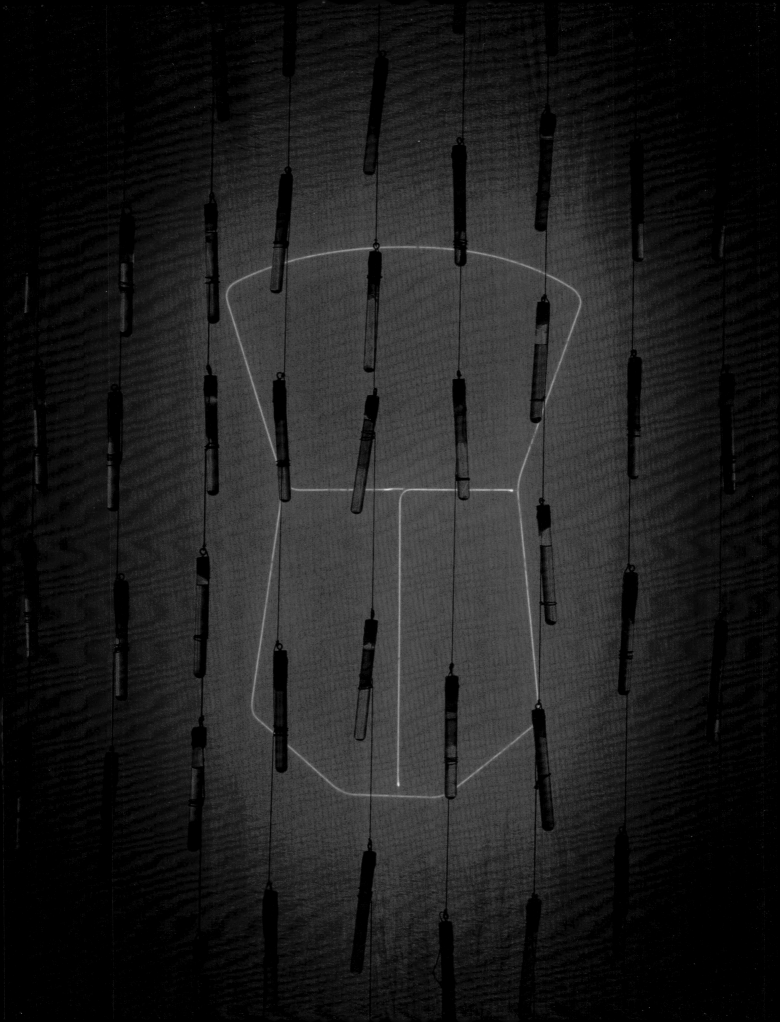

Storm Signals THE EITELJORG FELLOWSHIP AND NATIVE AMERICAN ART

"My art reflects our ability as indigenous people to retain our cultural heritage despite corporate and the U.S. Government standards of identification."
—TANIS MARIA S'EILTIN
(Tlingit)

"In a passionate confrontation with myth and history, images unfold and hint at the creative process."
—HARRY FONCESCA
(Maidu/Nisenan, Portuguese, Hawaiian)

68. Tanis Maria S'eiltin, *Resisting Acts of Distillation* (detail), 2002. Mixed media installation

The Eiteljorg Museum of American Indians and Western Art takes care to include at least one outsider more conversant with mainstream contemporary art than with the art and culture of Native Americans on the juries that select recipients of the Eiteljorg Fellowship for Native American Fine Art. That is how I became privileged to view a remarkable selection of works and bestow five $20,000 grants and an opportunity to exhibit at the museum on five gifted Fellows, as well as on the sculptor John Hoover, as Distinguished Artist. The museum also acquires work from its Fellowship exhibitions, so the project is triply rewarding.

The 2005 Fellows are the fourth group selected for this biennial event, launched in 1999 with the help of funds from the Lilly Endowment, Inc. In the catalogue for the 2001 exhibition, Jennifer Complo McNutt, the museum's curator of contemporary art, described the Fellowship's mission as providing Native American artists with the prospect of "greater influence and more visibility within the mainstream contemporary art world." She saw the awards as an opportunity to "dissolve the distinction between Native American contemporary fine artists and, simply, contemporary artists."

Until I visited the Eiteljorg, viewed the competing slides, and followed McNutt on two separate tours of the museum's astonishing contemporary collection, I assumed that the trajectory from indigenous to mainstream would not be very different for Native Americans than for other groups who have been challenging the dominant canon since the multicultural 1990s and the post-colonial era that ushered in the

millennium. In fact, there is much that contemporary Native American artists share with African-American artists, Asian-American artists, Latino-American artists, and even your common garden-variety, mainstream graduate of CalArts or the Yale School of Art. And that is a consciousness of the local and wider worlds in which they find themselves, and a sophistication about current artistic strategies such as performance, installation, conceptual analysis, appropriation, and sampling. Like artists of every stripe, they tend to be fluent in the languages that will most aptly permit them to express their issues of history, identity, nature, culture, politics, or spirituality. But, I have learned, there are also clear differences.

Fifteen years ago, *The Decade Show: Frameworks of Identity in the 1980s* sprawled across three Manhattan venues: The New Museum of Contemporary Art in the SoHo section of the city, The Studio Museum in Harlem, and the Museum of Contemporary Hispanic Art. *The Decade Show* announced to the mainstream art world that it was time to rethink such concepts as the "center" and the "margin," as Eunice Lipton wrote in the catalogue. Such a redefinition is yet to occur, but in fact the center did become slightly more porous, and the margins did begin to seep in. Some of the artists from that exhibit—including Edgar Heap of Birds, Jaune Quick to See Smith, Kaylynn Sullivan Two Trees, and Kay WalkingStick—have taught at the center, and at least a generation of artists and curators since, the cadences of their aesthetics and their concerns.

But what happened next for African-American and Latino-American artists

1. John Hoover, *Adam and Eve*, 1960. Oil on canvas

50. Harry Fonesca, *Winter Solitude #9*, 2003. Acrylic on canvas

has not, for the most part, happened for Native Americans. Very few American Indian artists have become members of the international art fraternity that populates the proliferating biennials, art fairs, and museums around the world. The Eiteljorg Fellowship is based on the assumption that the problem is structural, that if only Native Americans had the support that The Studio Museum, among others, has provided black artists for so many decades, Native artists, too, might now be considered "simply contemporary artists."

In the 1990s, so many African-American artists were finding their way into the mainstream gallery and museum system that the staff of The Studio Museum wondered whether it still had a role to play. Since then it has remade itself as a harbinger of artistic trends by focusing on the areas in which African-American artists lead the way, from investigating new ideas about hybridity in the 2001 exhibition *Freestyle,* to the blurring of the lines between folk and contemporary art in the 2005 exhibition, *Bill Traylor, William Edmondson, and the Modernist Impulse.* The latter exhibition caused the New York Times art critic Roberta Smith to write that "African-American folk art is as richly varied and innovative and important to American culture as blues and jazz."[1] In other words, The Studio Museum has positioned itself as an institution capable of redefining terms such as modernity and contemporaneity that have until now been enunciated by a largely white and European-influenced world.

Meanwhile, *New York Times* critic Holland Cotter pointed out that even

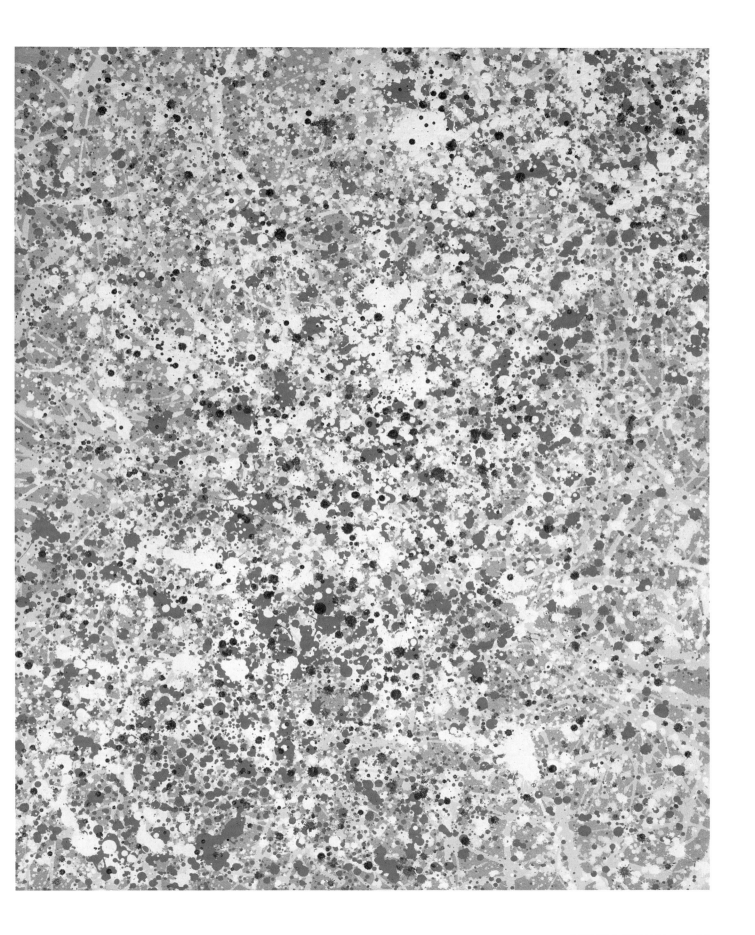

57. James Lavadour, *Deep Moon*, 2004. Oil on wood

the most conservative museums have been raising questions: "Whose vision of culture are we talking about anyway? Yours? Mine? Ours? Theirs? In the case of modern art, what makes West best?"[2]

An argument can be made that the Eiteljorg Fellowship can begin to do for Native Americans what museums like the Studio Museum have so successfully accomplished for African-American artists. Certainly, the prestige and money attached to the Fellowship can make a difference, particularly in the assurance with which the winning artists view themselves and are perceived as a result of the distinction, although excellent institutions have been concentrating on American Indian contemporary art for

some time now, in San Francisco, Phoenix, Santa Fe, and New York.

But I have come to believe that Native American artists are caught in a conundrum that differs significantly from the experience of other groups marginalized by the dominant artistic canon. And what the Eiteljorg Fellowships can do best is to give artists the time to ponder their aesthetic, intellectual, and emotional responses to the issues that face them in order to create statements so electrifying and so transformative that they reconfigure the conversation.

The other marginalized groups are immigrants, and when they look to their ancestral past, it is of another place, a different landscape. No one else has experienced the long-term systematic dis-membering of culture and history that fragmented the American Indian iden-tity, if only because African-Americans were brutally torn from one history and abruptly thrust into another. As for iden-tity, fragmentation is the modern condi-tion and the underlying assumption of contemporary art. But only American Indians are defined by the mathemati-cally precise percentage of Indian blood in their veins in the way that Hitler defined Jews.

There are reasons for these racial laws that many Indians embrace. It keeps imposters from exhibiting as Native American, without having endured the consequences of growing up Indian. Proof of authenticity is particularly important in a situation in which what institutional support there is comes from that very network of museums and gal-leries that focus on American Indians. The artists in this exhibition would not have survived without such a network. Even an established artist like Harry Foncesca—one of this year's Fellows who has shown in Austria, Germany, Japan, and the 1999 Venice Biennale—owes his career to a large extent to such institu-tions as the Heard Museum in Phoenix, American Indian Contemporary Arts in San Francisco, the Institute of American Indian Arts Museum in Santa Fe, and the National Museum of the American Indian in New York.

So the 1990 Indian Arts and Crafts Act, which demanded proof of Indian ancestry, seemed at the time to be a way of thwarting more than a century of U.S. laws that have stripped Native Americans of nearly everything by making new laws that entitle them to some of what is left.

This made it no less chilling to me, as the daughter of parents who fled Hitler and his racial laws, when I came upon the Certificate of Indian Blood that so many of these artists submit with their curriculum vitae and their slides.

And of course, comparatively few individuals are 100 percent Indian. Like Marie Watt, one of this year's Eiteljorg Fellows, they are "half cowboy and half Indian," as she puts it. (In her case, that means Seneca on her mother's side, German/Scottish on her father's.) Distinguished Artist John Hoover is one quarter Aleut. James Lavadour qualifies for enrollment in the Confederated Tribes of the Umatilla Reservation, where he lives, because he is $^2/_{32}$ WallaWalla, $^2/_{32}$ Assiniboine, and $^3/_{32}$ Chinook, the rest a mixture of French-Canadian trappers and German/Irish wheat farmers.

Tanis Maria S'eiltin, who is enrolled in the Alaska Native Claims Settlement as half Tlingit, can recite chapter and verse of her lineage as a member of the Shaa Hit, the L'uknaxa'di clan and the Yeil motley. But hers is an art that rails against the consequences of that 1971 Claims Settlement under which "aborigi-nal land claims were dissolved and $^1/_9$th of the state's land was granted to 13 regional and 200 village corporations."[3] The act, she points out, disenfranchised Indians born after 1971, among others, and left village corporations to struggle with their finite inheritance. And so her 2002 installation, *Resisting Acts of Distillation*, included a room filled with hanging vials of red liquid, audaciously defying interpretation and categorization. In juxtaposition with a room in which she had placed a deer-hide version of a mask long lodged in an anthopological museum, the installation was a dramatic visualization of what it means to be an Indian.

With their complicated bloodlines, Native American artists would seem to qualify as central casting's idea of the ultimate hybrids now so fashionable in biennals of contemporary art. But to be hybrid as it is currently defined by the mainstream museum world means to live in the Pop Culture moment, unfettered by the constraints of a particular history, free to create your own future by skimming the surfaces of other people's lives and ignoring the weight of your parent's suffering. Such hybridity, as the Harvard University postcolonial cultural theorist Homi K. Bhabha has articulated it, shuns oppressor/victim polarities in favor of a fluid state in which cultural history and "historic commonality" move back and forth, infecting and influencing one another in a present which is constantly moving toward the future that will define it.

This is hardly where the interests of the American Indian artists in this exhibition lie. They are passionately engaged in the enterprise of resurrecting what they can of their own history and systems of belief from the tattered remains of stories, memories, disinterred events, and reconstructed rituals. Whatever other nationalities they can calculate in their ancestry, and however small a fraction of Indian blood, it is the Native past that transfixes them. Edgar Heap of Birds, one of a handful of widely lauded Native artists, has made the obvious, outraged point that "the mark of the native experience cannot be measured in a blood fraction."[4]

And therein lies yet another irreconcilable contradiction in the snarl of conflicting signals from within and without that American Indian artists constantly must navigate. Their eyes are looking backwards while the mainstream-of-the-moment is in quest of the now and the what's next. But what of those artists who do find a language so convincing to the dominant culture that they are accepted by it? The cost can be enormous, both in self respect and in acceptance by their own community. Edgar Heap of Birds noticed that "when true Native American art is finally accepted, the style turns out to be that which fulfills the comfortable fantasy held by the non-Indian."[5]

James Lavadour, whose extraordinary grided variations on themes of creation, abstraction, and the landscape in this exhibition rehearse the workings of nature through his process of applying, building, scraping, and scumbling paint, has spoken about his art as "plugging into the 'big thing' as a way to get on the frequency (of the cosmos) and how to make connections with other people. It's not so much the cognitive ability of the artist to reflect," he said. "It's a very simple thing to be able to see through your culture, memory, and other finite things."[6]

But he was first noticed by the outside world in the 1980s when he made painterly figurative works that dealt with sex, alcohol, drugs, and the underside of reservation life. The artist Jasper Johns is not the only one who has noticed that when you find out what interests people about you, you tend to exaggerate it.[7] When Lavadour found himself playing the dysfunctional-Indian card for the

67. C. Maxx Stevens, *Three Graces* (detail), 2004. Mixed media installation

sake of mainstream popularity, he asked himself, "Is what I am doing worth doing?" He calls himself a self-taught artist despite his wide and deep knowledge in art, literature, and music. At that point, he took a hint from Albert Pinkham Ryder (1847–1917) and turned to the landscape he had hiked since childhood.

Those Indians who do decide to identify with the larger world that lionizes them are in danger of being dismissed as non-Indian by their community. That is how some in the Native world view Jimmy Durham, a darling of the international art circuit because of his ironic sculptural riffs on Indian stereotypes, who has moved away to Mexico and is no longer involved with Native concerns.

The issue of belonging—to family, community, history, and place—is incendiary. And so, many Native artists are torn between their allegiances and their aspirations, between how they are seen abroad and at home, between the imperative of reconstructing their shattered past and the perils of defining the future. They are like the angel of history that the philosopher Walter Benjamin imagined at the start of World War II:

His face is turned toward the past. Where we perceive a chain of events, he sees one single catastrophe which keeps piling wreckage upon wreckage and hurls it at his feet. The angel would like to stay, awaken the dead, and make whole what has been smashed. But a storm is blowing from Paradise; it has got caught in his wings with such violence that the angel can no longer close them. This storm irresistibly propels him into the future to which his back is turned, while the pile of debris before him grows skyward. This storm is what we call progress.[8]

How Native Americans deal with their dilemma to some extent depends on how old they are. There are generational differences in the ways in which the artists in this exhibition view their heritage, beginning with John Hoover, who was born in 1919. He is of the trailblazing generation whose lonely task it was to construct an identity out of stories read in books instead of heard in childhood and forms learned from spiritual objects isolated in museums. He was raised in the town of Cordova and went to public school, as the family tried to assimilate. He joined the U.S. Army, took Fred Astaire dance lessons on the G.I. Bill, earned his living as a commercial fisherman, and got his art training as a painter in Seattle, in the midst of a lively art scene spearheaded by Morris Graves and Mark Tobey. When he began making sculptures out of scraps of wood left over from the fifty-eight-foot boat *Aldebaran* that he constructed with a neighbor, he looked back to Aleut traditions, such as spirit boards, which were hinged panels that announced family, clan, and lineage.

"I was never lucky enough to experience any real traditional material. I had to read about it. Luckily, I was able to take traditional material and make it into my own vision,"[9] he has said.

The information he found was not always about Aleut art, but about general forms of shamanism, or ideas of transformation, or Native creation myths. These

he transformed into hinged tripartite sculptures, suggesting masks, totem poles or false house posts, and installations creating zones of mystery and awe. Out of disenfranchisement, he has sought out traditions not always his own, and made them whole and of his time through the language of stylization and modernism.

Harry Foncesca, born twenty-seven years after Hoover, in 1946, chose to graze the universal territory of myth and history through extensive travels in Germany, the South Pacific, Mexico, South America, Japan, and Italy. He fits his style to his subject, with the result that his paintings have ranged from gestural, to color field, to narrative, making them easily readable to a wider audience. However, this catholic attitude toward form has permitted him to probe such unhealed wounds as the effect on his ancestors of *The Discovery of Gold in California* (1999) in abraded canvases bleeding red, or the solitude of landscape in the all-over drips and impasto in *"Right" of Spring* (2003).

C. Maxx Stevens, born in 1951, identifies herself as a member of the Seminole Nation of the Oklahoma Region, and also, since she grew up in Wichita, as an "urban Indian." Because older artists like Hoover had already done the pioneering work of finding a place for universal Indian traditions in their art, she was early on advised to "know who you are. Don't do the kind of generic Indian art that's taken from different tribes."[10] Instead of the universal language of abstraction, she has specific stories to draw on, specific histories to investigate, like the 1830 Indian Removal Act, and specific questions to ask, such as "If you're urban, are you

Indian? If you're not, what are you?"[11]

Installations give her the ability to subtly layer her inquiry into the dense weave of politics, family, history, and loss that make up her art and her life, by building narratives of found objects or, in the case of *The Gatherers: Seven Sisters* (1999), employing the Native craft of basket weaving as a metaphor for the warp and woof of every species of intimacy.

Marie Watt, the youngest artist in the exhibition, was born nearly half a cen-

tury after Hoover, in 1967. She is an M.F.A. graduate of the Yale University School of Art in New Haven, one of the defining forces in the mainstream, though she took her A.F.A. in Museum Studies at the Institute of American Indian Arts in Santa Fe. Her latest works employ used blankets, which she stacks like totems or the *Endless Column* of Brancusi that announced the advent of modernist sculpture at the turn of another century. Her forms reference Jasper Johns, Louise Bourgeois, Agnes

77. Marie K. Watt, *Flag,* 2003.
Wool, satin binding, thread

Martin, Frank Stella, Kenneth Noland. The blanket sculptures and wall pieces are subtle, moving, and rich with every faceted connotation from the smallpox with which trade blankets decimated Indians to comfort on a winter night.

The bravura with which Watt negotiates the dualities between nature and culture, history and memory, inner and outer, ritual and daily life, community and post-modernity, rage, and the sweet revenge of pure invention is reminiscent of the mastery with which the Iranian-born artist Shirin Neshat taught the international mainstream to move over and make room for her. In the 1998 black and white video installation *Turbulent,* Neshat pitted a man on a floor-to-ceiling screen at one end of the room singing a love song by the thirteenth-century mystic and poet Rumi against a woman shrouded in a chador, on the other. And then the woman turned, and erupted in a song that drew on everything she had experienced as an Iranian woman, everything she had learned of possibility from avant garde composers such as John Cage, and transcended both.

When art does that, it becomes so powerful that it disrupts the stasis of mainstream and margins, changes the direction of the wind blowing from the past, unravels what had once seemed intractable, and clears a path toward a new realignment beyond polarities. And that is where the best of American Indian art has been going, in its own way and its own time.

NOTES

1. Roberta Smith, "Altered Views in the House of Modernism," *The New York Times,* April 28, 2005, section E, 31.

2. Holland Cotter, "Outside In," *The New York Times,* March 30, 2005, section G, 1.

3. Tanis Maria S'eiltin, quoted in "An Act of Resistance: Sacred Circle Gallery," *Art Access,* May 2002, 9.

4. Edgar Heap of Birds, "Sharp Rocks," in *Blasted Allegories: An Anthology of Writings by Contemporary Artists,* ed. Brian Wallis (New York: New Museum of Contemporary Art, 1987) 174.

5. Ibid, 171.

6. James Lavadour, quoted in Terry Toedtemeier, *Paintings that Kindle Joy: Conversations with James Lavadour,* catalogue for exhibition *James Lavadour: Intersections New Works,* at Maryhill Museum of Art, Goldendale, Washington, Sept. 7–Nov. 15, 2002.

7. Jasper Johns in conversation with Amei Wallach, early 1980s.

8. Walter Benjamin, "Theses on the Philosophy of History," [written 1940, first published 1950] in *Walter Benjamin Illuminations: Essays and Reflections,* ed. Hannah Arendt, trans. Harry Zohn (New York: Schocken, 1969), 257–58.

9. John Hoover, quoted in Julie Decker, *John Hoover Art & Life* (Anchorage: Anchorage Museum, 1985), 29.

10. C. Maxx Stevens, quoted in Gerald McMaster, "C. Maxx Stevens: If These Walls Could Talk, Environments that Tell Stories" in Gerald McMasters, *Reservation X: The Power of Place in Aboriginal Contemporary Art* (Seattle: University of Washington Press and Hull, Canadian Museum of Civilization, 1998), 149–156.

11. Ibid., 150.

John Hoover CARVING OUT A LIFE

JOHN HOOVER *(Aleut)*

Although he left the state some fifty years ago, John Jay Hoover and his artwork will be forever tied to Alaska, where he helped to redefine Alaskan Native art by embracing both tradition and innovation. The fragments of culture Hoover brings to his artwork are tales of shamans, spirit helpers, and the many animals revered by the ancient cultures of Alaska and the Northwest. His artworks are about transformation and nature and the animals he depicts are powerful, beautiful, and wise.

Hoover is nostalgic for a way of life he never knew and a people he has only learned of through books and museums. The stories Hoover draws upon to create his artwork have been passed down from generation to generation. As a descendent of the Aleuts, a culture devastated by Western contact and disease, Hoover did not have elders to tell him stories, so he set out to discover them for himself. To tell these stories visually, Hoover became a skilled carver and woodworker—a master.[1]

Hoover was born on October 13, 1919, in Cordova, Alaska, to a Dutch father and an Aleut mother, the youngest of three children. His father died of appendicitis while working on a mail boat in the Gulf of Alaska when Hoover was five years old and his mother supported the family by working in fisheries, mining camps, laundries, and oil fields.

Cordova was not a place concerned with tradition. It was a boom town, with new wealth and a diverse mix of people and industries. Located on Prince William Sound in the Gulf of Alaska, southeast of Anchorage, Cordova is a small fishing town, but it

was once the terminus of the Copper River and Northwestern Railroad, which carried copper ore from the Kennecott mine to the ocean. The building of the mine brought two or three thousand people to Cordova, making it Alaska's largest city during Hoover's childhood.

Hoover's public-school education was supplemented with piano lessons—music was an important part of the Hoover household. He also enjoyed visual art, taking classes in drawing and composition and experimenting with oil paintings. In grade school, Hoover frequently won American Legion poster contests, held every spring in Cordova.

Many painters visited Cordova in the 1920s and 1930s, including well-known artists of the Pacific Northwest such as Sydney Laurence, Ted Lambert, Jules Dahlager, and Eustace Ziegler. The painters, who were not permanent residents of Alaska but often came north to paint the grand Alaskan landscape, would gather in the evening and paint in the lobby of Cordova's grand Windsor Hotel, where Hoover would visit just to watch them paint.

Hoover took an extra year to finish high school, because he chose to dig clams rather than attend classes most springs, averaging one thousand pounds of clams in each tide and seventy-five dollars a day. After graduation in 1938, he worked at many odd jobs, including cannery worker, railroad tie tamper, pile driver, shipwright, machinist's helper, and taxicab driver. Fishing was the most consistent activity in Hoover's life and he even built his own boats. He also continued to experiment with oil painting. Although most of his paint-

18. *Seal Spirit Mask, 1989.*
Cedar

1. *Adam and Eve,* 1960. Oil on canvas

ings depicted images of fishing boats and the sea, Hoover did tackle many other themes and styles, and experimented with techniques of Cubism and Impressionism.

In 1952, Hoover, who was by now married with three children, left Cordova and moved to Washington state, first to Edmonds and later to Grapeview, where he still resides. There he became a member of Seattle Co-Arts, a group of painters who shared a gallery and who would go on painting excursions, most often to the waterfront. From 1957 to 1960, Hoover attended the Leon Derbyshire School of Fine Art, which specialized in drawing and paint-

ing and occupied the fourteenth floor of a Seattle high-rise. Hoover remembers brief interactions with other Seattle-area painters, such as Guy Anderson, Morris Graves, and Mark Tobey, who later became artists with international reputations. He says being in the continual presence of other artists helped him to stay dedicated to developing his own artwork. The paintings Hoover created during this time, in the late 1950s and early 1960s, varied in both theme and style. Most were reminiscences of his years in Cordova, such as *Trollers,* although others did reflect his current life and setting in Puget Sound, such as *Moon Trees I* and *II.*

2. *Trollers,* 1964. Oil on canvas

In 1958, Hoover and a neighbor built a fifty-eight-foot limit-seiner out of wood in Hoover's backyard. They lacked the proper power tools, however, and had to shape the timbers by hand. The boat, the *Aldebaran,* is still working out of Port Townsend, Washington, and building it made Hoover see possibilities for applying his woodworking skills to art.

While building the boat, Hoover would take small scraps of wood with wormholes and cut them into different shapes—not carving them, but cutting out rough figures and fish shapes. He would then hang them, like mobiles, from the ceiling of his studio, hinting at his later interest in creating large-scale sculptures that hung in space. He also practiced his woodworking skills by making traditional Aleut hunting hats, but rather than use the bentwood method typical of most Native craftsmen, Hoover carved his out of one piece of wood.

Hoover's first fully realized sculptures were oil-painted designs on cedar planks, inspired by traditional Aleut spirit boards, hinged decorated panels featuring an image representing a family, clan, lineage, or a high-ranking individual that is used during ceremonial performances. The figures in Hoover's works represented spirits, with simplified body forms and stick-like arms and hands. His use of color was minimal, with a whitewash delineating the figures. Cedar soon became his wood of choice, partly since it flourishes along the rain forest coast of the Pacific Northwest, but also because it is a very soft wood to carve.

Although his skill was improving,

Hoover began to resist the formal restrictions he thought came hand-in-hand with the formline style of the Northwest Coast art tradition. He stretched to find his own imagery and iconography. Hoover did keep some evidence of formline in his work in that most of his carvings include an outline that delineates the features of the animal or human figure he is representing. Most often, the outline is the raised part of the carving, creating what might be described as contour lines. The wood between the lines is carved lower and is usually a lighter shade, or another color altogether, than the lines themselves. Hoover kept Northwest Coast colors in his work, including red, white, black, blue, and green. He used artist oil colors and mixed them with turpentine and linseed oil. The additives thin the paint and create a stain-like substance that Hoover applied with a brush, later rubbing it in with a cloth until the grain showed through. Hoover's signature colors—washes of orange, rust, wood tones, the blue-greens of the sea—accent the natural tones of the red cedar. His work also alludes to the traditional Northwest Coast styles in his use of stylized images rather than naturalistic ones. As his work progressed, the images became more and more stylized and more and more recognizable as his own.

When Hoover was ready to move beyond the simple rectangular form of his early carvings, such as *Adam and Eve,* 1967, he began adding panels, hinging three separate planks together to create one unified work, such as in *Polar Bear Spirit,* 1971. The center panel was the largest, with two smaller side

panels which, when closed, would meet in the middle of the center panel. The panels were carved on both sides. The image shown when the panels were closed was different from the image revealed when the panels were open. This became one of Hoover's signatures. Eventually, almost all of his carvings would go beyond one single piece. The idea for creating diptychs and triptychs came from "traveling" Russian Orthodox icons, which folded up to protect the image inside.

As his carving skills improved, the complexity of these configurations increased. While he originally shaped his pieces like the icons, in the 1970s he began to cut his forms out. Now the carvings were identifiable outlines of real and mythical creatures. Instead of rectangles, the beak of a bird, the body of a woman, or the tusks of a walrus became three-dimensional shapes. As these cut-outs grew increasingly complex, as in *Hunting Scene Self Portrait,* 1988, so did their ability to transform when the hinged panels were open or closed. What in one formation was a pair of elegant loons on the exterior of a closed sculpture became a trio of spirit helpers when the piece was unfolded into its triptych state. Hoover has also experimented with creating asymmetrical forms, such as *Loon Lady,* 1994, adding still another layer to the folding and unfolding of his sculptures.

Hoover has explored other forms for his carvings as well, including mobiles, freestanding sculptures, simple mask forms, and mask forms with "appendages" attached with wooden sticks or pegs. Sometimes, small carvings will dangle from the ends of larger

carvings, such as *Heron Soul Catcher,* 2003, attached with bead-lined string or fishing line. Recently, Hoover has moved beyond his beloved cedar to work in bronze. One of his first bronze works was *Octopus Chimes,* 1981, a mobile. Despite the casting process, he still carves the original forms before taking them to local foundries.

Hoover's reinterpretations of Northwest Coast art gained him his first exhibition in 1968 at the Collectors Gallery in Bellevue, Washington, the validation he needed to continue as an artist. The Bureau of Indian Affairs purchased all but three pieces from the exhibition for its permanent collection. The remaining three sculptures were given as gifts to visiting dignitaries by President Lyndon B. Johnson. The Bureau's acquisitions became part of a traveling exhibition featured at the Edinburgh Arts Festival later the same year, the first time such work was shown outside the United States. The exhibition traveled to Berlin, Santiago, Buenos Aires, and Mexico City, as well as Anchorage, Alaska.

Thus began a very long career of solo and group exhibitions that eventually won Hoover an international reputation as an artist. In March 1971, Hoover's work was the subject of an exhibition at the Whatcom Museum of History and Industry in Bellingham, Washington. The exhibition was treated as a retrospective, even though it was the first time his work was the subject of a major museum exhibition. In 1973, Hoover participated in a two-person exhibition at the Heard Museum with painter Franklin Fireshaker, a Ponca painter from Ojai, California. The exhi-

5. *Polar Bear Spirit,* 1971. Cedar. Left, open; above, closed

bition was a critical point for Hoover. He was creating larger work than ever before, six- to eight-foot carvings of spirit birds, which he called "souls in flight," representations of a shaman's trance. The Heard Museum bought six works from the exhibition for its permanent collection.

In 1979, Hoover returned to Alaska for a solo exhibition at the Anchorage Museum of History and Art (he would have another exhibition there, a retrospective, in 2003). Hoover identifies this exhibition as one of his career highlights. The artwork presented in this exhibition—and later, in 1982, in *Night of the First Americans,* a one-night exhibition and reception hosted by the Kennedy Center in Washington, D.C.—was very symmetrical and stylized, demonstrating a maturity of style.

Hoover has received many awards and accolades. He received his first major award in 1972, a first-place in sculpture at the *Annual Contemporary Indian Art Exhibit* at Central Washington State College. He received a grant from the National Endowment for the Arts to teach sculpture at the Institute of American Indian Arts Museum in Santa Fe. His work was included in a permanent exhibition at the Institute that identified six innovators, defined as Native artists who drew upon their cultural heritage while using new materials, techniques, and designs. Hoover also traveled to Japan, Taiwan, and the Philippines as part of an artist-in-residence program that educated the children of men and women in the U.S. armed services.

In 1977, Hoover received his first public art commission, the beginning of what became an important outlet for his creativity. He created *Ancestor Figures,* an indoor sculpture, for the Daybreak Star Center in Seattle. In 1978, Hoover created a large mobile, measuring nine feet tall by nine feet wide, based on the supernatural being Sedna, the Great Goddess of the Alaska Inuit, or Inupiat, for the King County Alcoholic Center in Seattle. This was Hoover's first exploration of the mobile, a form with potential for animating a large public space that allowed him to move beyond two-dimensional wall hangings. In 1984, he was commissioned for what would become his favorite public art installation, *Volcano Woman,* installed at the William A. Egan Civic and Convention Center in Anchorage. In 1998, Hoover installed an enormous bronze sculpture, *Raven the Creator,* at the Native Heritage Center, also in Anchorage.

The range of subject matter found in Hoover's sculptures is broad, but some images play key roles, particularly that of the shaman. Many North American Indian myths concern the powers of the shaman. While in some the shaman inherits his or her role, he or she is more commonly summoned by the spirits, usually against his or her will, and driven into anguished isolation until he or she achieves enlightenment. When he or she then accepts the vocation, all the secrets of the universe are revealed to him or her and he or she begins a relationship with his or her spiritual aids and guides. Hoover is drawn to the mystique and power of the shaman, but is primarily interested in the ability of shamans to be vehicles for transformation. Hoover was also

very interested in the power of the female shaman, as demonstrated in *Woman Shaman Transforming into Her Eagle Spirit Helper,* 2000.

Birds, too, dominate Hoover's artwork, again for their ability to transform into spirit helpers. Perhaps the bird most commonly found in Hoover's work is the loon, a bird that regularly flies over Cordova and rests in the surrounding waters. The oral traditions of the Aleut, Inuit, and the Northwest Coast people include many stories about the loon that Hoover has depicted these stories in his artwork, such as in *Loon People,* 1996.

Loons served as guardian spirits to the Aleut shamans. A marine bird, the loon unites the worlds of sky and water. The loon's ability to bridge the two worlds makes it an ideal subject for transformation. Hoover also frequently depicts Raven (as in *In the Beginning Raven was White,* 1996, and *Raven Stealing the Stars,* 2001), a trickster common among many North American peoples. Other birds that appear in his work include cormorants, cranes, eagles, grebes, herons, hummingbirds, kingfishers, owls, puffins, and swans. Blue jays most often represent a self-portrait in Hoover's work, such as *Blue Jay Man, Self Portrait,* 1995, as Hoover closely identifies with the blue jay, a play on his middle name and the good humor he believes the jays possess.

Hoover also uses many northern mammals in his work, such as wolves, foxes, weasels, and polar bears. More often, he uses sea mammals—walruses, seals, whales, sea lions, and, particularly, sea otters. The Aleuts had at least eleven legends about the origin of the sea otter and many tales about hunting them. Figurines made of otters in the Aleutians were sometimes even used as adornments on the Aleut's kayaks. Abstracted images of otters were popular on traditional house posts of the Coast Salish people. Sea otters are believed to be important arbiters of morality and human behavior, withdrawing their support from hunters who do not honor their sacrifice. Hoover pays tribute to this history in works such as *Aleut Storyboard: Old Man of the Sea,* 1993 [not illustrated].

Almost all of Hoover's work incorporates some representation of human form. The faces in his work always hold the same expression (or lack thereof), inspired by Okvik Madonna figures, the small ivory figures that have been found scattered throughout Alaska and which are considered the oldest remnants of the Northern Maritime Culture, dating back to 300 B.C. The figures represent the spirit, or *inua.* *Inua* means "owner" or "indweller" to many North American peoples and the *inua* is the all-pervasive spirit with whom the shamans can communicate.

The faces and figures in Hoover's work are also symbolic of Native ancestors. Ancestors are very important in Alaska Native and Northwest Coast cultures. Full human figures may also be guardians, protective talismans, or personifications of environmental phenomena such as the sun. In most Northwest Coast art, when smaller animal figures are carved in relief on the cheeks or foreheads of human faces, the figures represent spirit helpers. The same is true in Hoover's work.

6. *Spirit Board,* 1973. Cedar

For Hoover, the feminine form is used to represent elemental sources of life. Hoover's literature on shamans revealed the awe women were held in for their ability to give birth to children. The shamans believed this ability gave women a secret of nature that men could never possess. Therefore, the human figures found in Hoover's work are almost always female.

Some of the images depicted in Hoover's work are not animals or people of this world. Instead, they are the supernatural beings. Salmon Woman (depicted in the *Salmon Woman* works from 1985, 1987, 1989, and 2001), is one of the more significant supernatural beings to inhabit the arctic region and the lower regions of the Northwest Coast, including Washington, Oregon, and northern California. Salmon Woman was a guardian spirit to both shaman and community. All along the coast, people's stories tell of Salmon Woman's gift of food for the people. Natives of the Northwest Coast and Alaska have depended upon salmon runs for food for centuries. Salmon are honored and celebrated by all coastal peoples. The fish serves as a powerful symbol of regeneration, self-sacrifice and perseverance.

Hoover's most recent work, including *In the Beginning Raven Was White,* 2001 (illustrated), typically features minimal color and further exploration with large, freestanding works, relying less on the diptych and triptych forms. Hidden among the ancient tales in Hoover's artwork is a much more personal story—the story of one man who has spent a lifetime creating, as an artist and a storyteller. Hoover calls his work "an obsession, something I have to do. If I'm not doing it, I don't feel whole. Sometimes I struggle, but it has got to come. Creating something makes you feel joyous, especially in the moment you are doing it." The Eiteljorg Fellowship is a fitting tribute to a lifelong dedication to a culture and a craft.

NOTE

1. For a comprehensive examination of Hoover's work, see Julie Decker, *John Hoover: Art & Life* (Anchorage and Seattle: Anchorage Museum of History in association with the University of Washington Press, 2003).

8. *Seal People,* 1975. Cedar

9. *Bird Woman (Dance Staff),* 1976. Bronze

10. *Loon Man Soul Catcher*, 1980. Cedar

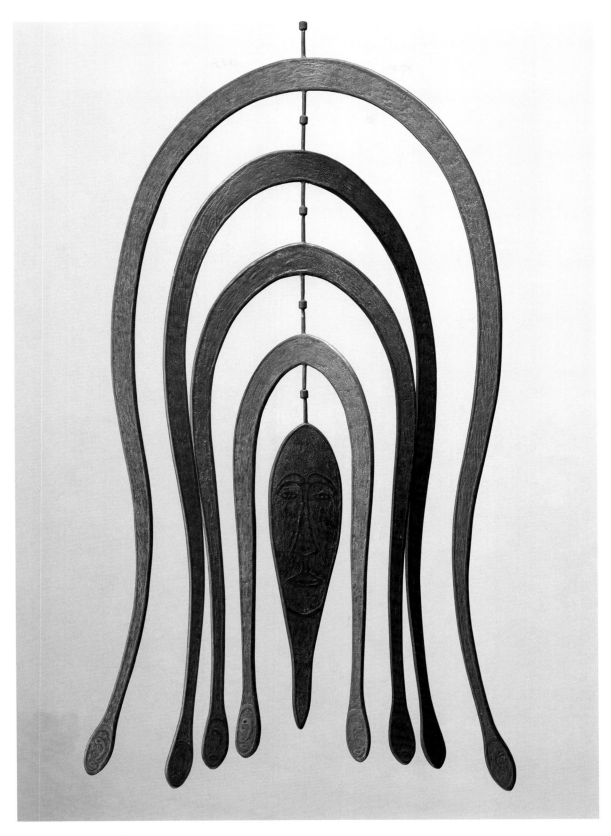

11. *Octopus Chimes,* 1981. Bronze

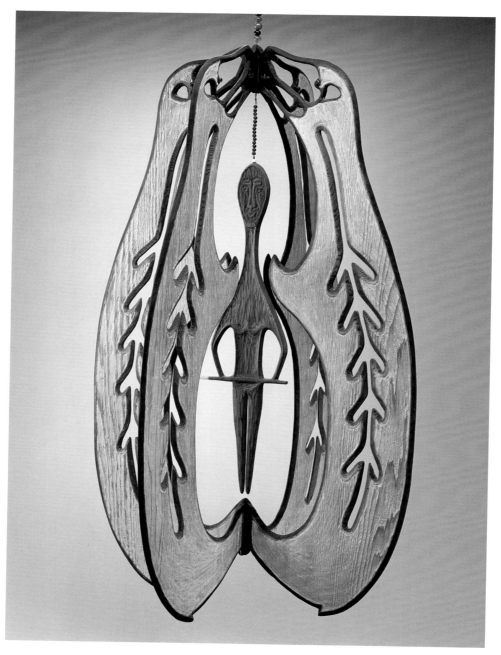

14. *Polar Bear Mobile,* 1987. Cedar

16. *Hunting Scene, Self Portrait,* 1988. Cedar

17. *Kushtaka,* 1988. Cedar

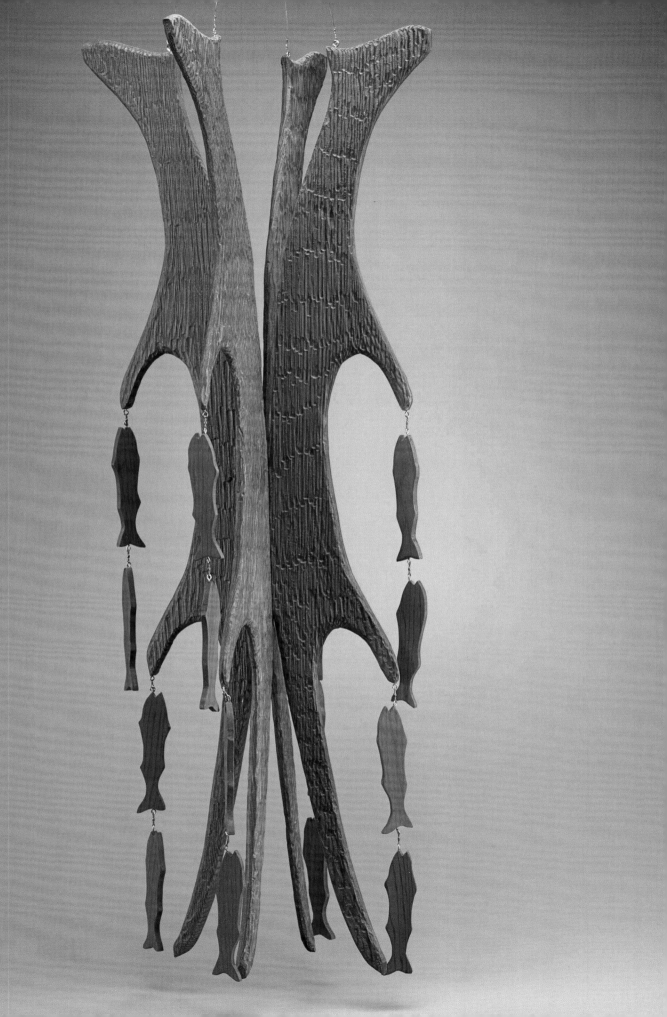

21. *Baby,* 1993. Cedar

23. *Loon Lady,* 1994. Cedar

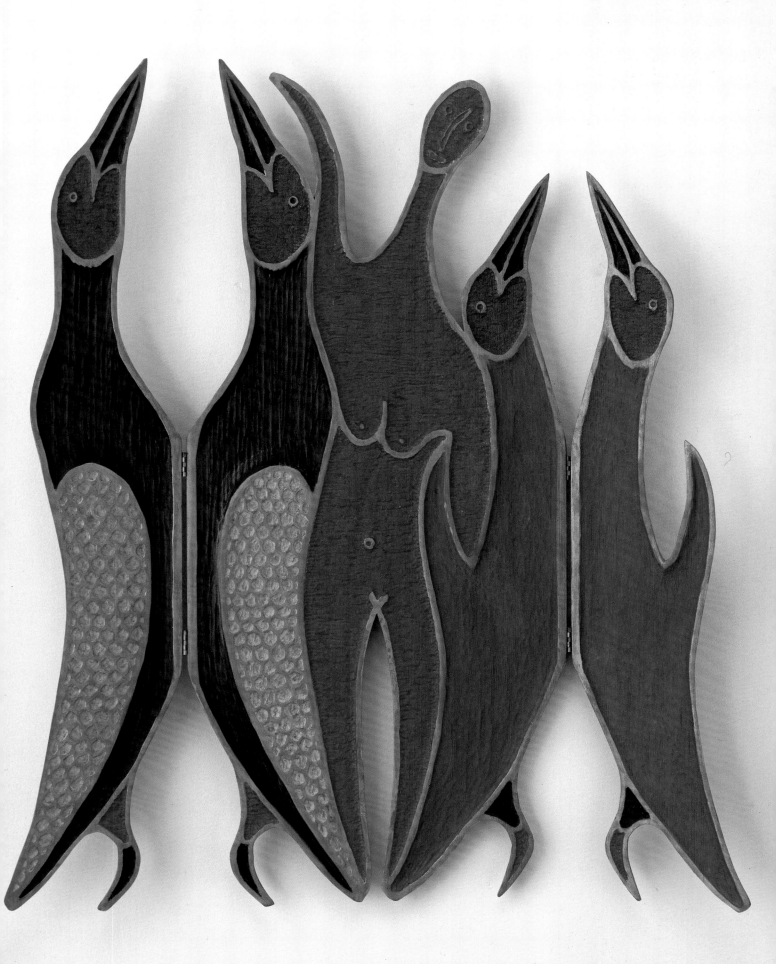

24. *Blue Jay Man, Self-Portrait,* 1995. Cedar

25. *Hummingbird Chimes,* ca. 1995. Bronze

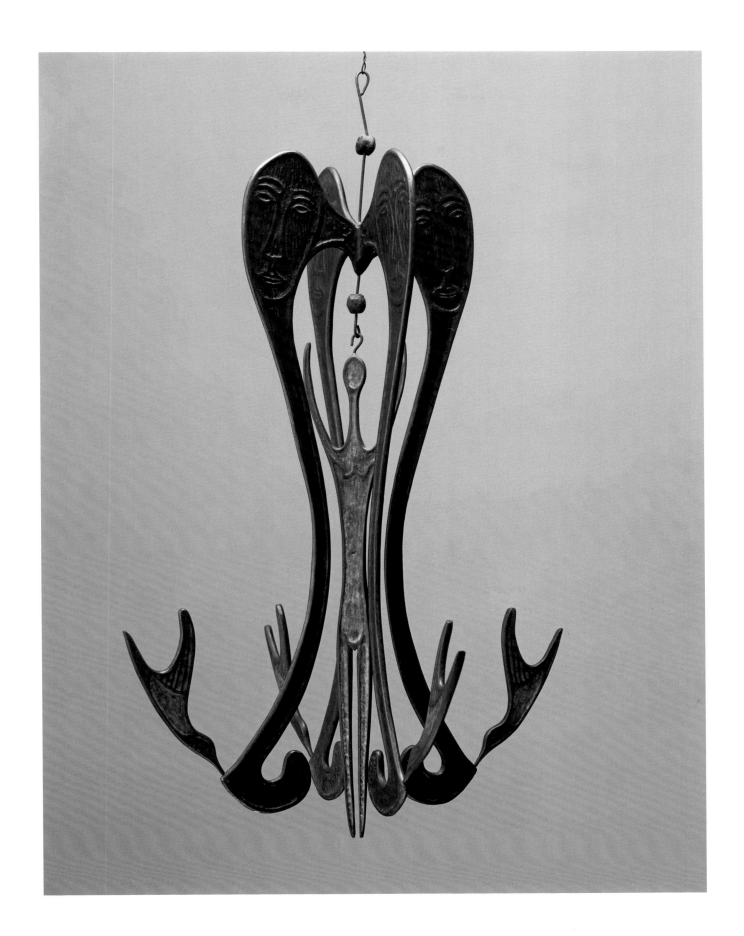

28. *Loon People,* 1996. Cedar

30. *Whale Family,* 1997. Cedar

31. *Blue Footed Boobies,* 1998. Cedar

33. *Sun,* ca. 1998. Bronze

34. *Moon,* ca. 1998. Bronze

36. *Woman Shaman Transforming into Her Eagle Spirit Helper,* 2000. Cedar

39. *In the Beginning Raven Was White,* 2001. Cedar

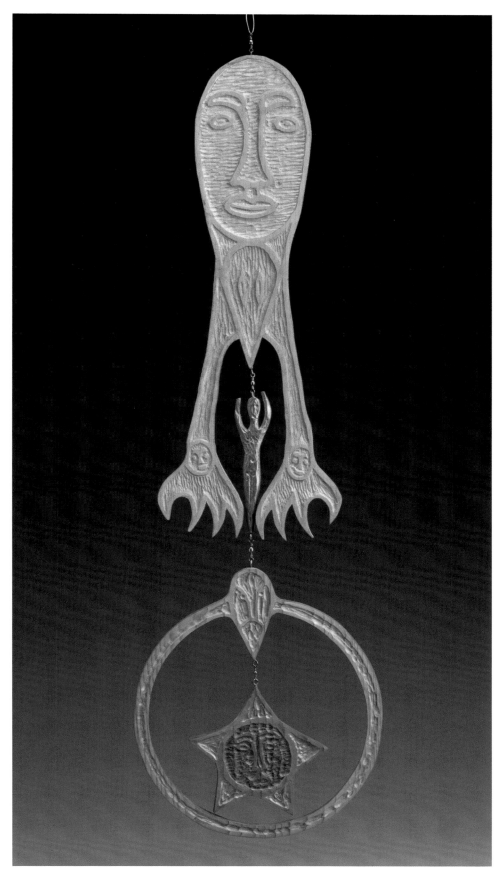

40. *Raven Stealing the Stars*, 2001. Cedar

42. *Heron Soul Catcher,* 2003. Cedar

43. *Copper River King, Copper River Queen, Princess Loud Mouth,* 2004. Cedar

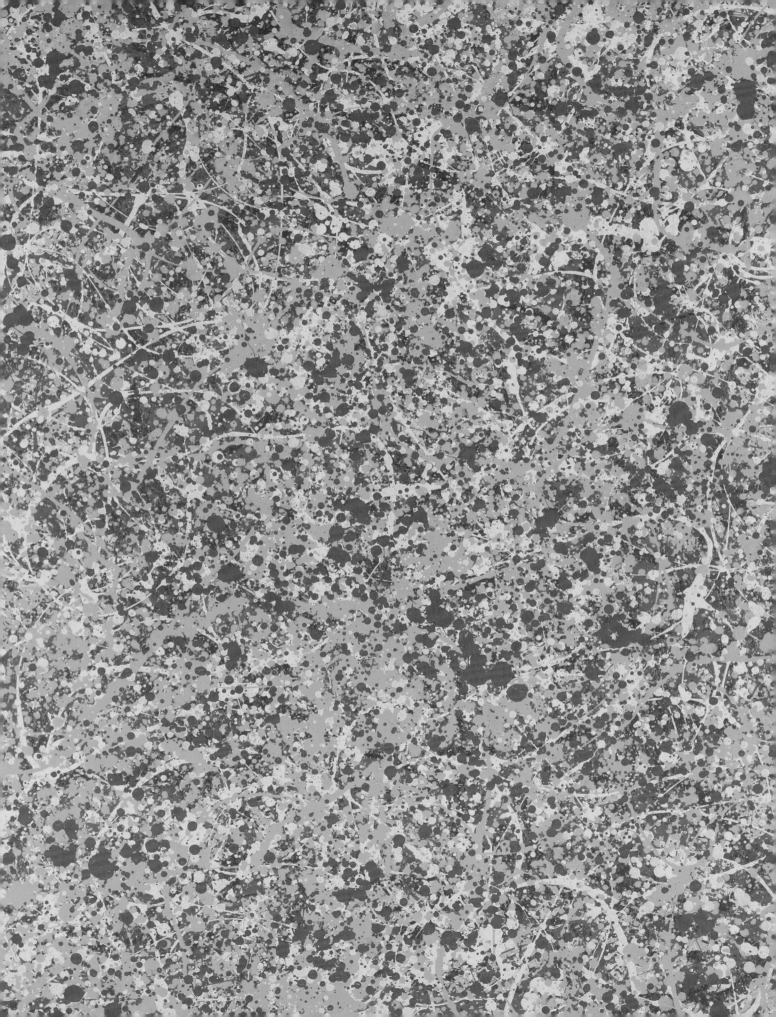

Harry Fonseca IN YOUR FACE, IN HIS ELEMENT

HARRY FONESCA
*(Maidu/Nisenan, Portuguese,
Hawaiian)*

45. *Autumn Sonata #30,* 2002. Acrylic
on canvas

Harry Fonseca has been a mover and shaker in the contested American Indian art world his entire career. In 1975, on the occasion of his first one-man show at Pacific-Western Traders, Folsom, California, I met a painter whose creative journey over the next thirty years would produce the kinds of virtuoso paintings that remain rare in the documented history of contemporary art by artists of Indian ancestry.[1] A force for change in the politicized arena of American Indian art, Fonseca is a quiet man, not willing to draw attention to himself outside the cultural arena, and hardly one to pontificate on the evolutionary course of modern art by practitioners of tribal origin. Instead, he uses his brush to state what some mainstream art scholars and critics have judiciously avoided in discussions of modern indigenous art practice—that quality is unmistakable, and great art is rare. Simply stated: Harry Fonseca produces great art.

Fonseca's work is a breath of fresh air in the quagmire that burdens the field of hyphenated/ethnic identity politics and that surrounds contemporary Native art and its criticism. He rarely stops to ponder the relevance of authenticity, representation, and authorship because for his work, these are non-issues. He is a man of convictions about the production of art, but his confidence is not based on a false sense of self-importance. Fonseca is one of a mere handful of art professionals on whom the mantle of significance is bestowed and he reflects this in his work. The Eiteljorg Museum's *Fellowship for Native American Fine Art* is well served by publicly acknowledg-

ing his tremendous creative influence in the field.

Of Nissinan Maidu ancestry, Fonseca was born on January 5, 1946, near the confluence of the American and Sacramento Rivers near the town of Bryte, California, on the outskirts of Sacramento. For the indigenous Maidu people, places where waters converge are important and imbued with power and magic. Although he remains close to his roots, Fonseca strides forward as a sophisticated citizen of the world through the minefield surrounding Indian art-makers. Many of his family still reside on the rancheria of Shingle Springs, while Fonseca elects to live and work in Santa Fe, New Mexico. His paintings are exhibited internationally and collected by major art institutions worldwide. As Fonseca emerged as an artist in the mid-1970s, the positive response to his work began to catapult him to the high-rise canyons of Manhattan where the art world is centered.

A graduate of the painting program at Sacramento State University, Fonseca earned an Master of Fine Arts degree. For a time, he was closely associated with two Native painters, themselves abstractionists, who taught in university art departments in California. Frank LaPena (Wintu) at Sacramento State, George Longfish (Seneca) at the University of California-Davis, and Fonseca formed a trio establishing the California Native art scene outside Santa Fe regionalism of the 1970s. Their disparate and respective styles were dominated by colorist imagery that Fonseca left behind by the early 1980s. Since the 1990s, Fonseca has

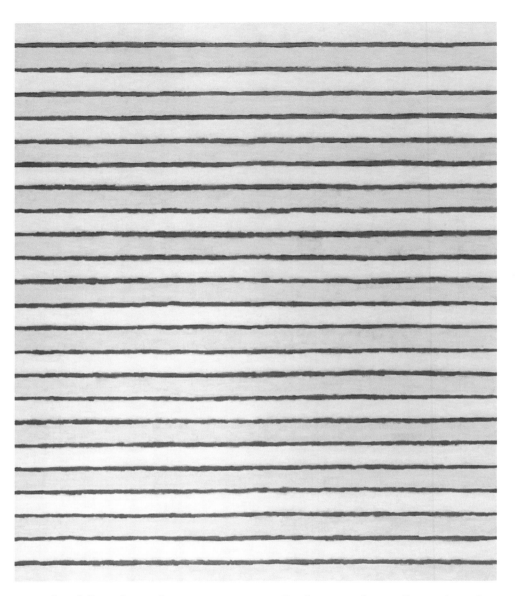

seemed to fully embrace the non-representational format most often associated with the New York School of abstraction in the late 1940s and 1950s. However, the recent works in the Eiteljorg exhibition reflect the processes that comprise Fonseca's serial examination of the physical properties of painting. Fonseca is never so exposed as when every line of color is clearly reflected and manipulated on the canvas. His work is an intimate window through which to view what separates him from others of lesser vision and innovation.

By the start of 2005, Fonseca's work had appeared in no less than four important exhibitions in Washington, D.C., including the Kennedy Center for the Performing Arts (*Night of the First Americans,* 1982), National Museum of Natural History (*Coyote: A Myth in the Making,* 1989), Ripley International Center (*Shared Visions: Native American Painters and Sculptors in the 20th Century,* 1993), and National Museum of the American Indian, George Gustav Heye Center, New York (*New Paintings,* 2003). Fonseca has exhibited no less than sixty-five times in

47. *Icarus #1*, 2002. Acrylic on canvas

California alone, and his work has been featured in Germany, Canada, Japan, and Switzerland.

Fonseca's inclusion in the majority of important touring exhibitions of contemporary Native art since 1975 attests to the considerable regard accorded to his work. Other significant one-man and group exhibitions include the prestigious XLVIII Annual *Esposizione Internazionale d'Arte,* Venice Biennale in Italy (1999); the landmark political response to the impact of the California gold rush on Native peoples, *The Discovery of Gold and Souls in California,* in Sacramento (1991–92); and *Stone Poems* in Los Angeles (1989). All were major introductions to Fonseca's evolving stylistic development, as he gradually moved away from his most recognized creation, the *Coyote,* and toward a new maturity. By the 1990s, Fonseca moved from California to Santa Fe at a time when national artistic and architectural interest centered on pueblo-influenced fashion and lifestyle. There, he noted that it was a welcome yet foreign setting that ultimately proved too confining to his evolving artistic vision. Observing that

48. *Requiem #1*, 2002. Acrylic on canvas

the more serious and elemental associa-tion of the coyote in California tribal mythology was overlooked through the rush to commodify the popular image, Fonseca withdrew from painting the popular character. The decision found him searching in new arenas with dra-matic results. Fonseca delved into more self-reflective and meditative works that announced a radical stylistic evolution in the appearance of his paintings.

By the start of the 1990s, Fonseca had introduced two experimental phases in his attention to the gestural action of the paintbrush—the visual record of the artist's hand in the paint-ing process. The first works from this serial process were *Stone Poems,* which revealed his continued interest in the archaic petroglyph rock art etched on the numerous outcroppings that litter the deserts of the ancient Southwest. Bold and vigorous in their layered sim-plicity, Fonseca's petroglyphic forms on unstretched canvases were, according to Lawrence Abbott, "not meant to be so much an interpretive recording of rock images but a way of self-exploration."[2]

A second series of serene and intro-spective works addressed both the sacred and the secular in an enigmatic and ambiguous figure of *St. Francis.* An assembly of haunting, singular, and centralized impressions of the saint conveys a meditative essence, perhaps an aura that emanates from him. Surrounded by serpents, or alone in architectural-like settings that harken to the Italian High Renaissance ideals, Fonseca's interpretations were moving him further from the commercialism of most Indian popular thematic art.

Fonseca acknowledged that his work is influenced by his extensive travels, primitivism, and the interactions with others. He is the first to acknowledge his powerful attraction to the tribal arts of Africa, Oceania, and Asia. Fonseca's deliberate and meticulous attention to color was the emotional marker of a deeper, perhaps dormant investigative process he had never before exposed to public scrutiny. Both of the above forms, however, signaled that the evolution was ongoing, a fact that has been fully realized with the current group of paintings for the Eiteljorg Fellowship exhibition.

From this linear progression, Fonseca drives toward a fully realized investigation of color, light, gesture, and structure with formalist intention.[3] He unveils yet another side to his creative processes with a group of color field canvases that may suggest to some observers the modernist American paintings of the last half of the twentieth century. In Fonseca's hands, these action-drip and color field works link him to several of the most important modernists painters of the twentieth century. Fonseca is an inheritor of the traditions of the western school of easel painting, and his acknowledgment of this connection breaks with the stereotypical notion some critics and Indian artists themselves have put forth that Natives create from an instinctual base, that it is "in the blood" rather than the product of education, formal and informal training, life, and practice.

The roots of abstraction have both indigenous and European sources, which are not in opposition. And while Fonseca was not the first to closely examine color in linear compositions, he has not rehashed the style as much he has reclaimed and restructured it.

In this exhibition, Fonseca's attention to horizontal format and linear elements of evenly spaced, hard-edged parallel bands incorporates a primary or a muted color palette that is minimalist and austere. Yet in *For Annie, A Poem After Poe,* 2004, Fonseca exposes that he cannot avoid his passion for color in the lower quarter of the canvas. An emphatic color band juts forth, creating a visual shock wave. It is a brash gesture carried out with one pinkish stripe contained between two purple-hued barriers and set against an overall modulated, alternating gray-on-gray backdrop. Fonseca returns to a minimalist palette with his austere *Illumination,* 2004, rendering tonal shades in primary colors. It is an unexpected approach brimming with freshness that emerges from the upper part of the canvas, where the brilliant yellow and orange-red become the focus of attention.

Fonseca's use of large blocks of primary color is not an overnight transition, but a slowly realized sequence to the fully abstracted interpretations in

49. *Right of Spring #20* (diptych), 2003. Acrylic on canvas

49. *Right of Spring #20* (diptych), 2003. Acrylic on canvas

51. *Red,* 2004. Acrylic on canvas

51. *Blue,* 2004. Acrylic on canvas

2004 with *Red, Blue, and Black.* Incorporating the three primary colors in an exercise that produces a known and comfortable palette, Fonseca returns to familiar terrain. He demonstrates his preference for a specific weighted color tonality, a recurring scheme observed in the earliest examples of his work, including the *Creation Myth, Coyote,* and *Stone Poems.*

One example of the earlier combination appeared in a series of Navajo blanket paintings on which he juxtaposed the drip painting technique.[4] But in his latest works, Fonseca has reduced this process to its the most elemental: the delineation of primary color upon secondary hues made visually alive with movement and texture, drawing the eye across the canvas in a trajectory that is familiar, left to right, top to bottom.

The evolution from the recognizable figural style of earlier forms, to the action drip style, reflects intensity and a somewhat introverted contemplation of the action involved in art-making. Yet, with the drip format, Fonseca relegates the physicality of the act of painting as his principal focus. He no longer is the author of stories in paint, but has transformed his thoughts to a more cerebral and concentrated process, the relationship of the hand and pigment, and its relationship to the surface of the canvas through the brushwork.

For some, action painting is most recognizable because of its association with Jackson Pollock's career in the late 1940s until the mid-50s. But Pollock's story is not Fonseca's. Jackson Rushing has pointed out the connection of the pioneer artist to the idea of the shamanistic curing ceremony.[5] Fonseca,

51. *Black*, 2004. Acrylic on canvas

with a playful hand and his use of pigment, builds the surface to draw the observer with him through a process that is visible in *Black Bird*, 2002. Fonseca allows the observer to follow his tracks as he builds and builds the surface with color that enchants rather than reflects the artistic angst so often associated with Pollock.

Observe how the themes of regeneration and renewal appear to dance across the canvas in celebration in *Right of Spring #20,* 2003, a diptych that overflows with the pinks and whites of a cherry blossom world akin to the Japanese nineteenth century Ukyoie woodcuts of Hiroshige. Fonseca has transformed the colors of the seasons to embrace the awe of the natural world. *Summer Dance #8* is Fonseca's interpretation of the glittering hot weather season. His insertion of golden hues of ochre and sienna against the white is

reminiscent of his *Crosses* series and the *Discovery of Gold in California.*

In *Autumn Sonata #30,* 2002, the warmth of the setting sun casts vivid orange-red steaks across the skies, and Fonseca seems to energize himself with activity. His energy is reflected in three works from his colorist roots. With *Winter Solitude #9,* the painter gazes outward toward the quiet snow flurry in a monochromatic rendering of white on gray. The seasonal calendar completed, Fonseca is alone with his thoughts, and audience and artist rest. In this sense, the dormancy is false, temporary, for we know Harry Fonseca is soon to embark on the next challenge and return with a new cycle and new vision. The anticipation is well worth the wait.

NOTES

1. I use the term to reference the tradition of easel painting in the western fine arts tradition of European-based "fine arts." That is to say, I am not referring to ethnographic traditions of painting by the indigenous cultures of the Americas.

2. Lawrence Abbott, "A Time of Visions," online at www.britesites.com, downloaded June 3, 2005, 10:34 P.M. from Netscape.

3. Aleta Ringlero, "Harry Fonseca," *American Indian,* 6, no. 1 (Spring 2005), 54.

4. I first viewed the Navajo rug series as preparatory sketches in 1989 in Harry's studio. Since this time, as curator of collections, I procured two of the series, *Variations on a Theme #13* and *Variations on a Theme #15,* for the corporate collection of Casino Arizona at Salt River, Scottsdale, a for-profit enterprise of the Salt River Pima-Maricopa Indian Community.

5. See W. Jackson Rushing, *Native American Art and the New York Avant-Garde* (Austin: University of Texas Press, 1995), 169–190.

52. *For Annie: A Poem After Poe,* 2004. Acrylic on canvas

53. *Illumination*, 2004. Acrylic on canvas

WHAT THE GROUND SAYS *The Art of James Lavadour*

JAMES LAVADOUR
(Walla Walla)

Now in his fourth decade as a painter and printmaker, James Lavadour is one of the most important American artists of his generation. His persistence, integrity, and commitment to craft have produced a stellar, if earthy, body of work characterized by grandeur, mystery, and sensuality. Mature and intelligent even in its earliest stages, Lavadour's art, which embodies the deepest engagement with nature imaginable, is kinetic and visionary. Both his imagery *and* his process are born of years of hiking the Blue Mountains of northeastern Oregon, which are his ostensible subject matter. His inner vision, which is a partner with the "body knowledge" acquired by walking ancestral land, is fueled by Native mythology, the Magic Realism of Latin American literature, the teachings of the Baha'i faith, and the ecstatic improvisations of jazz. Thus he commingles the intuitive and the concrete, the perceptual and the conceptual, and the emotional and the geological in majestic paintings that have secured a place for him in art history.

To witness such paintings as *Salamander,* 1997, or *Nest of Suns,* 1998, with their illusions of deep vistas, drifting fog, and craggy valleys, and their seemingly hard, wet, glistening surfaces that suggest Old Master painting, is to marvel that Lavadour has had no formal training in studio art whatsoever. Indeed, he describes himself as "a self taught modern artist living in a developing native Nation in eastern Oregon." That is, he still lives on the Umatilla Reservation where he grew up in a family "where everyone made or did something that could be called art,"

including drawing, music, beading, and weaving. And in addition to this legacy of creativity, the notion of "self-taught" must be qualified even further, as nature is a powerful mentor: "I learned to paint from being in the landscape."[1] Or, to paraphrase a nineteenth-century Cayuse Indian orator whom Lavadour admires, he listens to what the ground says.[2] He acknowledges the fact that family and community have been fundamental in shaping his art, and the Eiteljorg Fellowship jury was no doubt impressed by his cultural work, including nearly fifteen years of service to the Tribal Government in education, alcohol and drug treatment, and land-use planning. Perhaps his greatest achievement in community development, though, was as founder in 1990 of the Crow's Shadow Institute for the Arts, whose mission is "to provide social, economic and education opportunities to Native Americans through artistic development."[3] In addition to symposia on the economics of contemporary Native art, the institute organizes workshops for traditional arts and reservation youth. It also features a state-of-the-art fine art print studio, which has served distinguished visiting artists, such as former Eiteljorg Fellows Rick Bartow and Truman Lowe.

Since 1981, Lavadour's art has been featured in dozens of solo exhibitions, especially at university art museums, including the University of Oregon (1981, 1984), the University of California—Davis (1986), and the Pacific Northwest College of Art (1992, 1998). Other venues for one-man shows have included the Portland Art Museum (1990), the Sacred Circle

56. *Naming Tanager* (detail), 2001.
Oil on wood

Gallery in Seattle (1984, 1987, 1998), and the Northwest Museum of Arts and Culture in Spokane (2001). Even the short list of his group exhibitions is long, but several historic ones should be noted. In 1984, he participated in the legendary exhibition of contemporary Native art, *No Beads, No Trinkets,* at the Palais des Nations in Geneva, Switzerland. In 1987 the Portland Art Museum included him in *New Directions Northwest: Contemporary Native American Art.* I first became aware of his work when *Northwest X Southwest: Painted Fictions,* organized by the Palm Springs Desert Museum in 1990, was installed at The Blaffer Gallery at the University of Houston. In the catalogue of that show Lavadour wrote, "Whatever is in the earth, the world, humanity, is represented within me . . . . art must be the act of the heart to reconcile itself with the whole of being."[4] And in her essay, Iona Chelette located in his paintings "a modern metaphor with an original formal voice for relationship with earth forces."[5] The Heard Museum in Phoenix selected him for its groundbreaking exhibition, *Shared Visions: Native American Painters and Sculptors in the Twentieth Century* (1991), which was seen in numerous venues, including The Eiteljorg Museum and several museums in New Zealand.

Five large paintings, including *Under Fire,* 1990–91, were elegantly installed in *Land, Spirit, Power: First Nations at the National Gallery of Canada,* a significant Columbian Quincentenary show in 1992.[6] On that occasion, Lavadour produced an extremely thoughtful artist's statement that articulated with

impressive clarity a number issues that impinged (or not) on his artistic practice. It remains the most poignant textual manifestation of his art theory.

For many years now, my main preoccupation in art has been the investigation of a phenomenon in the process of painting that I call the "extraordinary event of nature." Rather than the depiction or representation of a specific landscape scene, my object has been to display the occurrence of landscape inherent in the act of painting. In paint there is hydrology, erosion, mass, gravity, mineral deposits, etc.; in me there is fire, energy, force, movement, dimension, and reflective awareness. For me landscape is not a picture, but a structure for a great experience. I use this structure to give form and identity to the vast and dynamic events that occur in the process of painting that are merely microcosms of the forces that shape the earth and the mountains. To paint is to engage with nature, and this engagement produces knowledge and the love of being.[7]

In my review of the exhibition, I wrote that Lavadour's paintings were "multi-panel paintings, with each panel conceived as a single word or event, which when assembled, make a poem." I also noted that "for me these painterly poems evoke a turtle-skin tectonics characterized by primordial mud slides, vaporous clouds of algae and moss, and fiery blood on the mountainside."[8] In retrospect, the overriding quality of *Under Fire* and the other paintings in *Land, Spirit, Power,* including *Star,* 1990–91, strikes me as a *visceral grace.* More recently, Lavadour was included in *Indian Time: Art in the New Millenium* at the Institute of American

54. *Bridge,* 2001. Oil on wood

Indian Arts Museum in Santa Fe in 1999 and in the *2003 Oregon Biennial* at the Portland Art Museum.

The strength of Lavadour's exhibition history is furthered validated by numerous commissions for public art projects by the Washington State Arts Commission (1982, 1985, 1987), the Seattle Arts Commission (1983), and the Oregon Art Commission (2000). A selected list of his honors and awards also confirms widespread interest in his art. The most recent of these was a Flintridge Foundation Award in 2004,

55. *Garden,* 2001. Oil on wood

preceded by his being named an Honorary Doctor of Humane Letters by Eastern Oregon University in 1999. He was the recipient in 1998 of a coveted Joan Mitchell Award, given by the foundation established in New York City by the brilliant if iconoclastic Abstract Expressionist painter, who shared Lavadour's poetic enthusiasm for landscape. Twice he has been a Fellow at the Rutgers Center for Innovative Print and Paper (1990, 1995), and relatively early in his career he benefited from an Oregon Arts Fellowship (1986).

Lavadour began his journey as an artist in 1969–70, and even his earliest work, such as an abstraction made with food coloring on paper completed in 1972, reveals his penchant for what the critic Vicki Halper described as "a sub-

tractive method of depiction, and an exploitation of the physical properties of his materials."[9] On the surface—so to speak—the paintings that established his critical reputation are "Romantic landscapes." But that is an oversimplification, as indicated by various critical discourses, including his own. Writing in *Art in America* in 1990, Ron Glowen saw "primordial nature as the true subject of the paintings." And yet, he recognized that "within this elemental scene, incipient skeletal or spectral figures rise from the basaltic mass."[10] Glowen may well have had in mind such works as *Thunderhead and Bloody Face,* 1987, or *Seed,* 1988, in which Lavadour has "figured" the land, calling attention to mountains, valleys, and rivers as the site of both myth and history. Chelette, too, realized that Lavadour was subjecting "nature" to "anthropomorphic transformations."[11] Writing for the Portland Art Museum, Prudence Roberts also made landscape-as-subject contingent: "Certain rocks take on the look of skull and teeth; skeletons can be seen in the sheared-off cliffs and truncated torsoes [sic], birds and animals discerned in these mysterious vistas. . . . Clearly, these scenes have as much to do with internal as with external verities of land."[12] Note that Roberts distinguished between land and landscape, the latter being a pictorial convention. Charlotte Townsend-Gault underscored this distinction by comparing the sweep of Lavadour's painterly gesture with the "sweep of the bare basalt hills outside his studio," stating that such gestures "implicate the artist with land, not the landscape."[13] Besides, Lavadour self-describes as an "abstract action painter," who just happens "to see landscape in the abstract events of paint."[14] And although he admits being interested in Albert Bierstadt and Albert Pinkham Ryder, he, too, wants to interrogate the category "Romantic Landscape":

I want to steal the words "Romantic Landscape" away from our bloody American history and clothe them with new meaning. Something like . . . "where vision is always arriving like a river." You may put your feet in and let the current tell you of mountains and hidden places. They should be words that stretch like a lake to receive every new outpouring of possibility and shed light on the unseen.[15]

Who or what are these "restless spirits"[16] that possess or are possessed by the land, and which were frequently seen in his paintings from the mid-1980s through the early 1990s? The oral history Lavadour learned as a child animated the land: places had names, were the sites of memorable events. In particular, a regional origin myth involving Coyote suggests that the blood, bones, and monstrous images in *Boom!,* 1988, for example, constitute the iconography of creation.[17] Halper proposes that such imagery might represent the displacement of "personal and cultural demons" into the land from *their* origins in the figurative interior scenes that mark his "cathartic" period (c. 1983–86).[18] These "interiors," as he calls them, are haunted and haunting expressionist images of apparitional figures in compressed interior spaces. *Sheds Light,* 1983, which was exhibited at The Heard Museum, and *Reservation Voodoo,* 1985, for example, are aesthetically violent, and in them we see sex, death, grief, psychic dislocation, fractured bits of symbols, and architectonic distortions. They pictorialize loss, grief, and estrangement, and give form to Lavadour's assertion that "living in a community like the reservation, all the ghosts are present."[19] As recently as 1998, he made three paintings titled *Ghosts of Ceded Boundaries,* which do not feature anthropomorphic imagery and which must surely refer to colonization and land loss. Ultimately, though, he grew weary of the fear expressed in the "interiors." This disenchantment, coupled with his 1986 encounters with the Grand Canyon and with Ryder's eerie landscapes, clarified his intentions, and he began to forge what we might call his signature style. He explained this shift in an artist statement in 1989: "In Indian country, art is used to rise above despair, not to provoke it. Its purpose is not progress, but the simple and repetitious reaffirmation of identity, relationship, and place."[20]

Lavadour's rededication to landscape and to an art of affirmation also meant returning to an experimental process of discovery. By the mid-1980s, then, he was committed to mastering what he understood as the language of painting, and virtually *all* serious critics of his work have noted his deep investment in process. This attention to the qualities of paint and the requisite picture support runs parallel to Lavadour's insistence that he does not care what his paintings mean, but rather, what they do and how they do it. But this, in fact, is one of the modernist ways of explaining how the audience has access to meaning: through its awareness of the creative process. Collectively, his critics have recognized wiping, scumbling, blotting, thinning, scraping, slurring, layering, and stippling as ways in which he manipulates pigment and surface. Similarly, in an effort to find through his process the event of nature he locates both in the land and in himself, Lavadour has used a variety of picture supports: masonite, gessoed cotton canvas or wood, clay paper on wood panel, linen, birch veneer, and paper on board.[21] His working method is the Abstract Expressionist one, and we should note that he shares their interest in the Beat poets and jazz as a model for creativity.[22] That is, like Jackson Pollock, he identifies with nature, insisting that he wants to internalize it, not merely represent it. And like

Willem deKooning, he finds his subject matter/image in the working process. In particular, he employs a strategy, used at times by Adolph Gottlieb, Philip Guston, and Mark Rothko, of creating by thinning, scraping, and wiping away layers already put down.[23] The endgame of this improvisational process is always unknown, and for Lavadour "it's a process of acquiring information and knowledge from kinetic experience."[24] As with the Abstract Expressionists, the journey of studio practice is its own reward: "I am searching for something. In painting as in nature there are worlds to discover."[25]

The four twenty-first-century oil-on-wood paintings selected for the Fellowship exhibition are proof positive that Lavadour's search and discovery process continues to evolve. *Naming Tanager*, 2001, is "classic" Lavadour, the grand summation of almost fifteen years of painting: sixteen autonomous panels assembled in a grid formation six feet wide by eight feet high. The title and palette are intertwined, as the colors of the western Tanager serve as a metonym for sweat lodge stories about the first naming of the animals.[26] The "events of nature"—volcanic fire, jutting promontories, the twisting Snake River—are kith and kin, but the imagery is discontinuous, if stunningly expansive. Some critics have identified a cinematic sensibility in such a format, but if so, it is the dream-like deconstruction of filmic narrative, or as he noted, "a lot of times my landscape stretches just like in your dream."[27] Hazy forms appear, disappear, and reappear, while a whispery mist and a scorching fire alternately paint the sky.

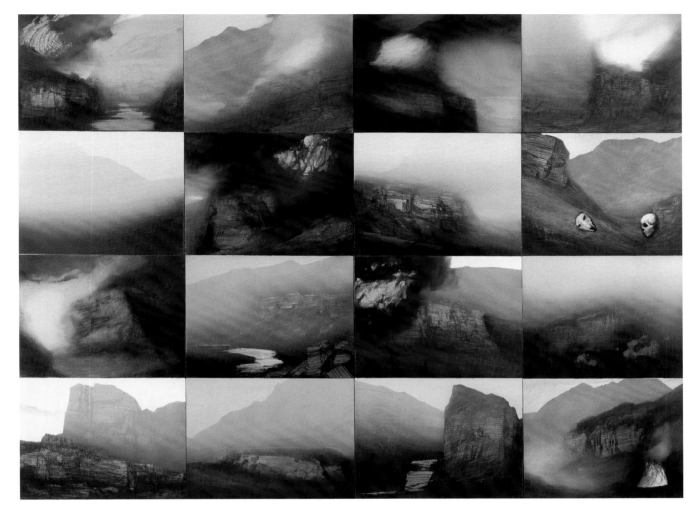

56. *Naming Tanager*, 2001. Oil on wood

Black shadows and a thin yellow light are dyadic partners, and in spite of the individuality of the panels, the whole of the painting builds inexorably up through the center like a mountain. The only trace of human presence, save the record of the artist's gesture, are two partially unearthed skull fragments near top right, which resemble theater masks, emphasizing the surging drama playing out before us. So, as Lavadour asks, what does it do? For me, it makes time—the glacial pace of geologic formation and the vicarious time insinuated by the record of a painterly performance—which is, perhaps, the mind of space, damn near tangible.[28]

Bridge, 2001 represents a new direction that began in Lavadour's work in 2000. His experience as a printmaker had encouraged him to be more analytical about his process and structure:

I broadened my palette, my composition and even my thinking. I had worked at abstract and landscape at the same time. I called them [the "pure" abstractions which he exhibited c. 1999–200] *interiors* and landscapes . . . . They used to go parallel, but now they integrate and intersect. That was a major technical and psychological breakthrough for me.[29]

The processual change is simple enough, but the results are anything but. He began to take the underpaintings for landscape panels and turn them upside down and work on them with different tools, creating a more architectural painting, gestural but faceted, on

57. *Deep Moon*, 2004. Oil on wood

Deep Moon (detail)

top of it. When assembled into their final geometric configuration, sometimes the panels stay "upside down," so that gravity is defied and the rivery drips run uphill. The effect of this transformation of his "operating system" was a "startling discovery" and extremely energizing for him. *Bridge,* whose core panel of icy, angular shards of geometry seems sheared off by some unseen force, is far more unstable and dynamic than *Naming Tanager.* The difference is not in quality, but in effect, as his newer "methodology" is an even more determined fusion of internal and external realities.

The black-green palette of *Garden,*

2001—think thinned out motor oil— has been seen elsewhere in his oeuvre, including in *Ghosts of Ceded Boundaries I, II, and III,* 1998, and in the intimate, sketch-like paintings on clay paper exhibited in *Native Paper,* a group exhibition I organized at Gallery 210 in 1996 at the University of Missouri-St. Louis, with Lavadour, Phil Young, and former Eiteljorg Fellows Joe Fedderson and Kay WalkingStick. But now, with a greater awareness of physics, Lavadour is exploring flow, cosmic vortex, and turbulence. Borrowing from the Rutgers University physicist Norman J. Zibowsky, he now understands and speaks of the long,

running drips of thinned pigment not just in terms of gravity, but also "fingering instability."[30]

Deep Moon, 2004, a nine-panel painting six feet wide and nearly eight feet high, shows us where he has been most recently. The process-driven image speaks more than ever of the subjective logic of artistic vision. Color is freed from the job of evoking nature as seen, implying instead the mind's eye, as it witnesses tectonic forms in raspberry, midnight blue, and fibrous hemp green. A decorative, almost stylized raking of the surface created striations that hint at blanket patterns, wave forms, or the shuddering earth, quaking in a spasm of delight at its own convulsive energy. This force—whatever it is—has dispersed color in a pulsing point/counterpoint of hot and cool, with some panels clinging to the surface, while the center panel drifts away from us into a dreamlike space, reminding me of a line by the poet Robert Hass: "Longing, we say, because desire is full of such endless distances."[31]

In recent conversations, Lavadour has spoken with enthusiasm about this new path in his artistic journey and about the influences he is absorbing, such as the musical traditions of India. Sketching has become central to his method, he feels newly liberated in terms of form and color, and speaks with passion about an even greater striving for universality.[32] In particular, he continues to be nourished by the writings and teachings of the Baha'i faith. Halper has written with clarity about this relationship, and suffice it here to note that the impact of the Baha'i faith reveals itself in certain titles and themes in his art and certainly in his personal philosophy and art theory.[33] Mark Tobey, the Northwest modernist whose "white writing" has a central place in the spiritual history of twentieth-century art, was likewise deeply inspired by Baha'i traditions. Lavadour's art is complex and points in different directions simultaneously, including toward the geometric designs native to the Columbia Plateau and to the nature-mysticism-abstraction tradition embodied in Tobey's work and that of such Northwest visionaries as Guy Anderson, Kenneth Callahan, and Morris Graves.[34] But if comparisons must be made, and indeed they must, if only to remind us that art, like nature, is an interdependent web of relationships, then Lavadour's art may be favorably compared to George Morrison, who was honored posthumously by The Eiteljorg Museum in 1999. Morrison, too, was a process-oriented painter, inspired by land, water, and sky, and his compelling visions of Lake Superior and its environs sang to their audience much the way Lavadour's paintings do. And yet, Lavadour is only at mid-career and it is far too early to situate him, as many miles of painting stretch out before him: "I am now a mature person fully engaged with my talents and faculties living in the homeland that I love. This is the time of my life I have been working for. How long can it last? I want to make some good paintings while I am able."[35]

NOTES

1. James Lavadour, undated artist statement, courtesy of the Eitlejorg Museum.

2. See James Lavadour, artist statement in Diana Nemiroff, Robert Houle, and Charlotte Townsend-Gault, *Land, Spirit, Power: First Nations at the National Gallery of Canada* (Ottawa: National Gallery of Canada, 1992), 180.

3. See note 1 above.

4. James Lavadour, quoted in Iona Chelette, "Northwest Narrative Painters," in Katherine Plake Hough, et al., *Northwest X Southwest: Painted Fictions* (Palm Springs Desert Museum, 1990), 17. Other artists in the show included Guy Anderson, Robert Colescott, and Jacob Lawrence.

5. Chelette, "Northwest Narrative Painters," 17.

6. See W. Jackson Rushing, "Contingent Histories, Aesthetic Politics," *New Art Examiner* 20 (March 1993): 14–20.

7. James Lavadour, artist statement in *Land, Spirit, Power,* 180.

8. Rushing, "Contingent Histories," 20.

9. Vicki Halper, *James Lavadour: Landscapes* (Seattle: University of Washington Press, 2001, for the Northwest Museum of Arts and Culture), 14. Halper's essay, to which I am indebted, is the most comprehensive overview to date.

10. Rob Glowen, "James Lavadour at Cliff Michel," *Art in America* 78 (December 1990): 177.

11. Chelette, "Northwest Narrative Painters," 17.

12. Prudence Roberts, *Northwest Viewpoints: James Lavadour* (Portland Art Museum, 1990), n.p.

13. Charlotte Townsend-Gault, "Kinds of Knowing," in *Land, Spirit, Power,* 94.

14. See note 1.

15. Ibid.

16. Lynn Smallwood, "James Lavadour at Cliff Michel," *Artnews* 90 (January 1991): 168.

17. Halpert, *Lavadour,* 11–12.

18. Ibid., 20.

19. James Lavadour, quoted in ibid., 18.

20. James Lavadour, quoted in Patterson Sims, *Crossed Cultures: Five Contemporary Artists* (Seattle Art Museum, 1989); see Halper, *Lavadour,* 20.

21. Cf. Halper, *Lavadour,* 24, n.9.

22. See, for example, his comments in Daniel Gibson, "James Lavadour," *Native Peoples,* vol. 8 (September/October 2000): 46.

23. Michael H. Lewis, whose mystical landscape abstractions are to Coastal Maine what Lavadour's are to the Plateau country, generates imagery through an oil wash on ragboard with turpentine. Working independently, Lavadour and Lewis have arrived at similar aesthetic solutions for dealing with internal and external "spirit-land." See Carl Little, "Michael H. Lewis at the University of Maine Museum of Art," *Art in America,* vol. 78 (September 1990): 203.

24. James Lavadour, quoted in Gibson, "Lavadour," 45.

25. James Lavadour, artist statement in *Indian Time: Art in the New Millenium* (Santa Fe: Institute of American Indian Arts Museum, 2000), n.p. On Lavadour and Abstract Expressionism, see also Halper, *Lavadour,* 15–16

26. Personal communication, July 23, 2005.

27. James Lavadour, quoted in Halper, *Lavadour,* 23.

28. *Time is the Mind of Space, Space is the Body of Time* is the title of a three-panel painting (1982) by the mystical Abstract Expressionist Richard Pousette-Dart; see Maurice Tuchman, et.al., *The Spiritual In Art: Abstract Painting, 1890–1985* (New York: Abbeville Press for the Los Angeles County Museum of Art, 1986), 351.

29. James Lavadour, quoted in Eva Lake, "The Event of Painting: An Interview with James Lavadour," www.lovelake.org/event_of_painting_James_Lavadoutr.htm

30. Ibid.

31. Robert Hass, "Meditation at Lagunitas," in his volume *Praise* (New York: Ecco Press, 1979).

32. Personal communication, July 15, 2005.

33. See Halper, *Lavadour,* 16–17; Roberts, "Northwest Viewpoints," n.p.; and Lavadour, in *Land, Spirit, Power,* 181.

34. This is not to say that Lavadour has been influenced by this Northwest mystical modernism, but rather that he shares certain of its inclinations and aspirations. See Sheryl Conkelton and Laura Landau, *Northwest Mythologies: The Interactions of Mark Tobey, Morris Graves, Kenneth Callahan, and Guy Anderson* (Seattle: University of Washington Press, 2003).

35. See note 1.

STORIES FROM THE HEART *The Art of C. Maxx Stevens*

C. MAXX STEVENS
*(Seminole/Muscogee Nations
of the Oklahoma Region*

*"I tend to return to the fam-
ily in my work . . . how we
are connected, how we relate
to each other. . . . it is who I
am."*

—C. MAXX STEVENS

63. *Book Ends: Memories of
Childhood* (detail), 2004. Book, mixed
media

C. Maxx Stevens was born in Wewoka, Oklahoma. She is a member of the Eufaula Band of the Seminole Nation. Her family moved to Wichita, Kansas, when she was five years old, at a time when many Native American families were relocating to urban areas for work.

"My family moved to an area of Wichita called Plainview. This area was a deserted Air Force base housing complex from World War II. The government sold the leftover barracks to low income families. From the Oklahoma and Kansas regions, many native people were being relocated to Wichita to work in the airplane plants, so many of these families purchased these homes from the government. This created a Pan-Indian community."[1]

Stevens pursued her interest in sculpture at Haskell Indian Junior College and after receiving both an Associate of Arts and a degree in Indian Arts Studies. She was encouraged by her mentor, Dr. Richard West, Sr., to continue her art education. Stevens re-entered college and received a Bachelor of Fine Arts degree in sculpture and ceramics from Wichita State University, along with a Metals Certificate from the United Welding Institute and a Master of Fine Arts degree in sculpture from Indiana University. While at Indiana University, she began working in theater design, ultimately perfecting her use of lighting and space, which she continues to incorporate into her installation pieces.

"It was with working with the lighting designer and the set designer that I really began to understand 'space' and how light can affect a piece, and how you can control your audience—even

from that movement from one position to another within the work itself, through the lighting of the pieces along with the placement of the art," Stevens states.

Stevens has been an educator at the Rhode Island School of Design, School of the Art Institute of Chicago, and the Institute of American Indian Arts and Culture, as well as an associate dean at the White Mountain Academy of the Arts in Canada and dean for the Center of Arts and Cultural Studies at the Institute of American Indian Art.

As you walk through the spaces that Stevens has created within the confines of the installation area, you are brought into her personal world of family, memory, and individuality. Delicate baskets hover in midair, somehow relating to each other and yet standing alone in their own serenity. Billowing dresses of tissue as ephemeral as butterfly wings are laden with iconographic imagery of loved ones, Raven, places, hearts, Cheshire cats, raw meat, and disassociated hands, faces, and feet. Books are open to pages with faded symbols upon them portraying everything from childlike drawings to old portraits.

Stevens is a master storyteller and key artist in the current Native art movement and her installation work is solidly situated within the contemporary art world. Her works have been shown at the Boise Art Museum, Tribe Art Gallery, Mobius Gallery, National Museum of the American Indian, Smithsonian Institution, Museum of First Civilization, the Museum of Art and Culture at the University of Montana, Missoula, the Heard Museum,

Gorman Museum, and the Institute of American Indian Arts Museum.

Stevens' installation pieces have covered an array of Native American issues including the Indian boarding school experience (*If These Walls Could Talk*[2]) and the impact of Christianity upon indigenous communities and religion (*Four Directional Houses*[3]). Most often, however, they refer to personal topics of family, memory, identity, and sense of history and "place" within a Seminole context. In these particular pieces, Stevens explores her own individuality as she delves into the matriarchal family structure of her culture and depicts its honored status as it has molded her sense of identity and self worth.

Stevens characterizes herself as a "visual storyteller" and it is a befitting description of her art process. "I recollect my memories and the stories I grew up with, my lineage, my family, my foundation of my art work. The way I'm able to communicate is through the art form of installations. Presenting concepts with the use of materials and space; the materials and objects are like words, putting them together to produce a statement or story."[4]

Stevens layers a multitude of images within her pieces, and these images act as metaphors and allegorical statements. At first sight, art pieces such as those in *The Three Graces,* 2004, may appear perplexing, no more than a confusion of photos pasted onto an amorphous ball. But very little examination is needed to reveal deep and thoughtful meaning. Family portraits are juxtaposed against pictures of ravens and such incongruous images as ladders lead the eye up and around to the indi-vidual crowning icon at the pinnacle of each paper gown.

Although the colors and textures of her installations are often subdued, the overall effect is a distinct feeling of warmth and comfort. The materials she uses are organic in nature and feel. In Stevens' earlier works, she often used metal, utilizing her welding skills to fabricate her artwork, but she has recently turned to the use of vines, branches, and twine, erecting frameworks for coverings of tissue and wax paper.

As the light plays down upon the installation pieces, the illuminated paper glows softly and throws off a warm yellow color into the surrounding areas. In *The Three Graces,* Stevens admits us to a matriarchal story of the three elder sisters of her family. She describes the honored status that being the oldest women holds within her family:

In the society that we are from, the women are the head of the family and they are the ones who sit together to make family decisions. And so we happen to have a lot more power, and have a strong voice about what happens with the family structure. My mother and my sisters, we tend to be the ones who gather at the kitchen table and make decisions, and talk about things that have happened. And others are not allowed to sit with us at certain times. . . . it's not even spoken, it's just common knowledge. It is a tradition, and we three sisters seem to have taken our place at that table.

The installation consists of three dresses, each a representation of the three eldest sisters: Lou, Molly, and Maxx. The dresses are constructed of branches lashed together and covered

58. *Gatherers: Seven Sisters*, 2000.
Mixed media installation

with paper, giving them a sense of delicate frailty. Stevens "yellows" the translucent paper with a technique of her own design and then builds upon the structure layer by layer. In Lou's piece, the images are iconographic, representing Lou as the assembler of family information. Lou is the sister that the family contacts for information about each other. Like her dress, Lou embodies the total assemblage of family information. Upon the dress are photos of the family, both current and past, of their mother and grandparents, of siblings, of the crow which represents "storyteller" and "traveler," and on top sits an icon of "home."

Molly's dress is very graceful in construction and materials. Horsehair and storybooks encircle the waist area, referring to Molly's strength and talent as the verbal storyteller in the family. "Molly is elegant, and beautiful, and is a wonderful speaker." The bottom is trimmed with hundreds of ID tags. "I like the notion that we all have to have a way of identifying ourselves, and so I decided to make the ruffle out of these tags." Within the center of Molly's bodice sits a picture of their mother

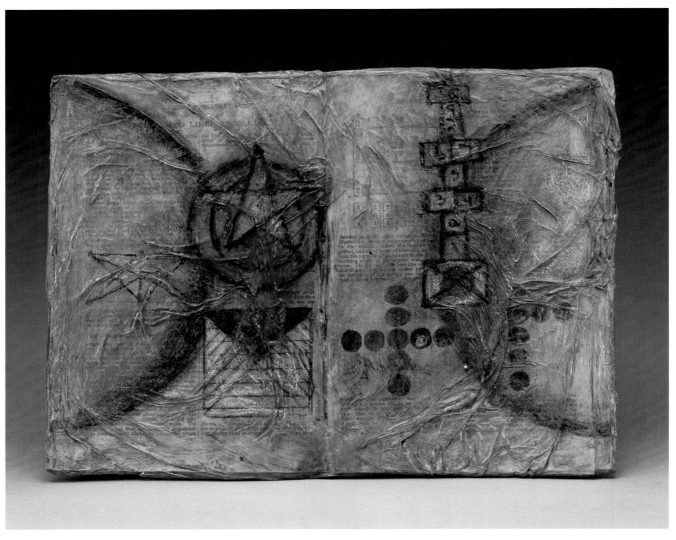

59. *Book Ends: AI Is Between the Two Moons and on the Star,* 2004. Book, mixed media

and her parents—the heart of all three sisters. Stevens describes Molly as the "caretaker of the family," and in this piece she has erected a protective enclosure around Molly's heart.

Stevens constructed her own dress with the "fabric" on the inside. The delicate paper of the dress can be seen through the vines. "I am hard to get to know, but once you get past the hard layers, there I am," she says with a smile. The ribbon work of her dress drapes over the lashed structure. "This is me . . . kind of like who I am. My style is quite different from theirs. A little bit more raw. In the piece that represents me, the vines are exposed, the paper is not perfect . . . but at the same time, there is a more 'revealing' of who I am." And at the top is a staircase, leading up to a photo of her mother, her grandparents, and herself. This center is protected by a barricade of twigs. "There are boundaries set around the inner me, and it takes a bit of effort to get to know me."

60. *Book Ends: As It Should Be,* 2004. Book, mixed media

Gatherers: Seven Sisters, 2000, depicts the siblings of Stevens' family. Their relationship to each other is conveyed by the placement of the baskets within the room, each basket reflecting individual aspects of each family member. Some sit just a little off from the group, emphasizing a strong sense of individualism, and some are closer to the core. They seem not to suspend isolated, but rather to evolve around a central area—their place of origin. Stevens describes their relationship to one another:

In a family of nine, the older one [sic] are more separated in age than the others. The eldest, our brother, is a bit more separated from the elder sisters in age. Because of the wide age differences, there are different levels within our family . . . in how they relate to each other. Because the age separations range from seven years difference to thirty-one years difference, there are just inherent differences in the way that we relate to each other.

Stevens' *Book Ends* is a much more personal art piece. Five books lie open

61. *Book Ends: Centering*, 2004.
Book, mixed media

to the audience, and within the pages are stories, glimpses, into her life. Ladders represent artistic and personal growth, pages about close friends, and about growing up in the barracks of Planeville, Kansas, and playing on ancient swing sets. One book is opened to images of beloved and honored family members. "You see those portraits that honor famous people. . . . I placed those whom *I* honor in that context." When asked about why one image is scribbled out, Stevens replied, "Well, that represents those who have been historically honored in that way, who haven't deserved it."

What memories these installations represent we cannot and *need* not know. The enigma of these objects does not isolate them, but rather evokes a sense of a communal connection. *What* memories we have, we have individually. *That* we have them is what we have in common. Our own memories are integral to us as persons—that we all have them is integral to us as a com-

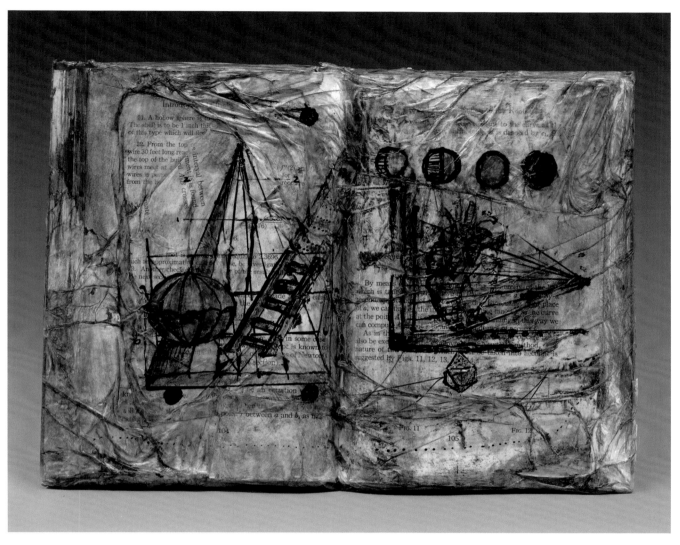

62. *Book Ends: Complexity,* 2004.
Book, mixed media

munity. C. Maxx Stevens continues to provoke audience responses with a depth and insight to what it means to gather stories from the heart.

NOTES

1. From the upcoming C. N. Gorman Museum exhibition, *Bodies & Circles.*
2. *Reservation X* exhibition, 1998, First Civilization Museum, Hull, Quebec, Canada.
3. *Contemporary Native American Art: Reflections After Lewis and Clark* exhibition, 2005, Museum of Art and Culture, University of Montana, Missoula.
4. Excerpt from the upcoming C. N. Gorman Museum exhibit *Bodies & Circles.*

63. *Book Ends: Memories of Childhood,* 2004. Book, mixed media

64. *Book Ends: Process of Thought,* 2004. Book, mixed media

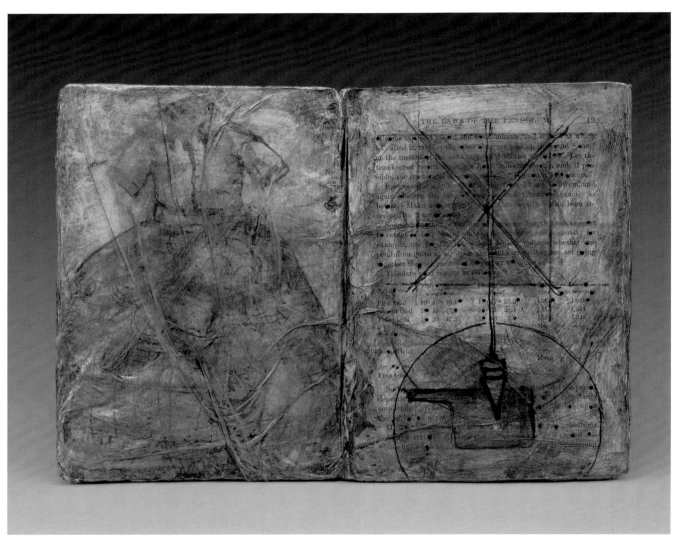

65. *Book Ends: Red Portrait,* 2004. Book, mixed media

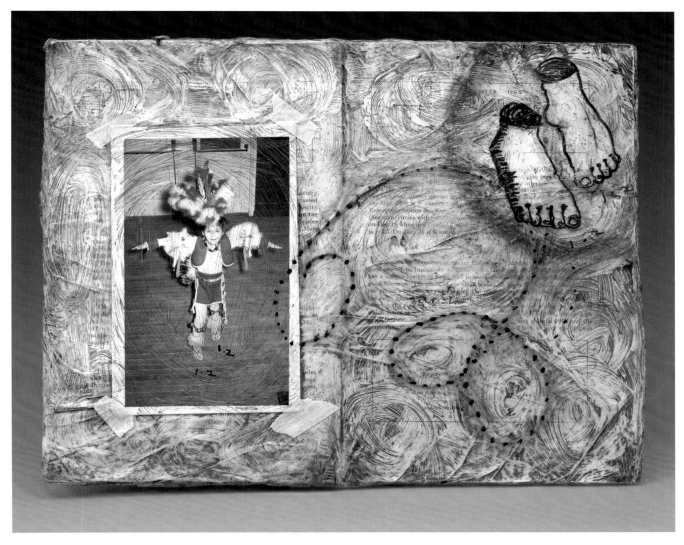

66. *Book Ends: Shunatona Dance Steps,* 2004. Book, mixed media

67. *Three Graces*, 2004. Mixed media installation

67. *Three Graces* (detail)

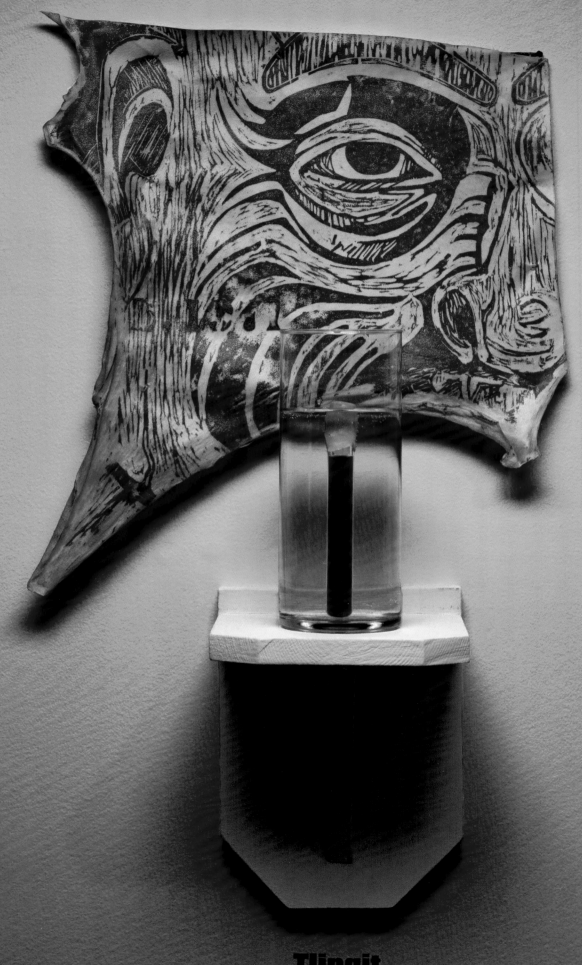

Tlingit

Tanis Maria S'eiltin COMING FULL CIRCLE

TANIS MARIA S'EILTIN
(Tlingit)

Tanis Maria S'eiltin was born in Skagway, Alaska into the Tlingit nation, Yeil (Raven) moiety, L'uknaxadi (Coho) clan, and a family of artists. Raised in a culturally rich environment of story-telling and creative activity, S'eiltin was surrounded by the artwork of her mother, Maria Joseph Miller, who cre-ated moccasins, boots, purses, parkas and, later in life, was a master weaver of Chilkat Blankets. Learning from her mother's exacting standards of perfec-tion, she began picking up piecework for her mother. Back then, the young Tanis Maria did not consider herself, nor her mother or uncles as "artists"—instead they were creating pieces for the community and non-native consumers. In apprenticeship with her mother, S'eiltin learned to bead and sew work-ing with fur, skin, and hide as a regular part of her childhood.

Living in Skagway, Alaska, she recalls the frequent trips to Klukwan and the thirty-four-mile ferry ride to Haines that she, aged nine, and her mother would take to visit with aunts, uncles, and grandmothers, for which she would sometimes barter her fare in fresh salmon. She witnessed the storytelling that was so memorable in her child-hood and the fluency with which her mother spoke the Tlingit language.

Inspired and encouraged by her mother, S'eiltin attended the University of Alaska in Fairbanks where she earned a Bachelor of Fine Arts in printmaking in 1986. As in so many fine arts educa-tions, S'eiltin was instructed through the narrow, hegemonic framework of western art history that consistently excludes and dismisses the rich Native cultural capital she had developed

68. *Resisting Acts of Distillation,* 2002. Mixed media installation

throughout her life. Influenced by the "Greenberg concept of art," her masks and prints were abstract, "non-objective," and without cultural rele-vance.[1] Shifting her focus from two-dimensional pieces to sculptural objects, S'eiltin began incorporating found materials and continued to create abstract works, though she was starting to reveal undertones of cultural reference.

While completing her Master of Fine Arts degree at the University of Arizona in Tucson in 1992, S'eiltin was inspired by the political artworks cre-ated by her fellow Latino/a students. "At that time I was questioning the rel-evance of fine art and realized that con-temporary art could contribute to soci-ety as traditional Native art has always done, in the past and present. I realized that using media for its aesthetic quali-ties as a visual hook, and basing the manipulation of that material on a political narrative, I could definitely make art that would educate my audi-ence."

Her academic research about Native American experiences in the Southwest paralleled the historical knowledge she held about similar experiences on the Pacific Coast. Missionaries, colonialism, old world diseases, so-called "pio-neers"—her people had long-endured them as well. S'eiltin's research emerged through her thesis exhibition, marking a personal and professional turning point in her artistic career. In the series of large, fifteen-foot-tall drawings, she addressed issues of conquest and expressed the enduring strength of indigenous peoples. It was then that she first questioned mainstream America's

68. *Resisting Acts of Distillation* (detail), 2002. Mixed media installation

perception of Native art by challenging the categorization of indigenous art, as either craft or artifact, and began creating contemporary art that actively defies the imposition of western labeling.

Armed with both the knowledge of western art theory, and a solid founda-

tion of indigenous art knowledge, S'eiltin began creating works that challenged hegemonic references and stereotypes while considering contemporary approaches to indigenous art-making practices. Her exploration of abstract and western art practices empowered and strengthened her perspective of Native American art, and eventually led to an artistic reunion with her mother. In 1995, S'eiltin exhibited her paintings alongside her mother's weavings to convey "social statements concerning identity issues" at the Sacred Circle Gallery in Seattle.

In the *Savage Apparel,* 2004, series, S'eiltin brings together her indigenous and academic knowledge to create works that query preconceived notions of Native art and apparel. At first sight, the pieces are faintly reminiscent of purses or containers but instead S'eiltin's combination of materials and creative techniques cultivate a sense of inquiry.

By utilizing natural materials such as beeswax, hornet hives, bear claws, and whale baleen, as well as fur, skin, and hides, S'eiltin returns to some of the materials of her youth. She explains how working with fur, skin, and hides "just seems like a natural process. I don't have to spend a lot of time questioning how I'm going to use the materials, manipulating it becomes automatic. Creative problems are easily solved because of past knowledge of the material."

Yet, she employs the materials in an entirely unique way by purposefully challenging herself to break the rules and guidelines she has been taught both by her mother and in printmaking. She playfully combines the natural materials with found objects, industrial materials, non-art objects, and marine supplies. Intrigued by the form of a wire-rubberized crab-bait box with its lids and latches, she works spontaneously stitching materials together with the box as the base. In response to the careful and precise stitching she learned with her mother, she intentionally breaks the rules of skin sewing by exposing the stitches and knots.

My work is not as refined as my Mother's, not as well crafted because she held different standards for her work. I can remember working with her for hours and having to redo things because they weren't correct and that was how she was taught. The pieces in the *Savage Apparel* series were in response to those types of lessons where everything had to be perfect. Creating *Savage Apparel* was an intuitive and playful response to regimented creative activities that were encouraged by my Mother and academia.

By alluding to more traditional pieces, yet distinguishing her works by her use of materials and technical construction, S'eiltin intentionally "counters, by emulating, the stereotypical view that mainstream America has about Native American art—about beads, feathers, rawhide, and crudeness."

If the idea is that Native artists produce only crude and primitive crafts then that is what will be made . . . but with a twist! I think about how to challenge or emphasize those stereotypical notions about Native American art. I want to work crudely, so I employ rawhide and smoked fish hide, and whatever media is intriguing at the time. I just start playing with the materials and the bait boxes—and they take on their own form. I try to let go of any aesthetic parameters I hold and just play. The twist is that a stereotypical object looks Native in design, is made of hide and fur, hinting at traditional regalia and skin-work, but cannot be identified as a functional object.

More than hinting at tradition, and celebrated for their functionality, are the exquisite drums in the series entitled *War Heads,* 2003. Created in collaboration with her brother, Tim Ackerman, the large, forty-four inch hand-drums resonate with a rich deep bass sound when they are played, actively carrying back the war helmet S'eiltin has printed on the raw hide.

When naval lieutenant George Thornton Emmons acquired the Tlingit war helmet from Dry Bay, a village just south Yakutat, Alaska, in 1888–93, he could not have envisioned how, more than a century later, his actions would motivate and inspire an empowered Tlingit artist to bring the helmet home. Now sitting in the American Museum of Natural History in New York City, the helmet is one of 2,500 pieces that Emmons sold to the museum in 1894 for $25,000.[2]

Until its physical return to S'eiltin's grandmother's village, the artist commemorates the piece through memory and visual repatriation. In remembering the piece, she recalls how she has "always appreciated its beauty from the time I was a child until now. Once I got involved in drawing it and making the woodcut, I appreciated it even more. I would really like to know who the artist was who created it." S'eiltin's indigenous view comes from a knowledge and closeness with artwork from her community, interpreting and acknowledging the skill of the artist and exceptional design.

While in grade school, S'eiltin became discouraged by the academic descriptions and research about coastal artwork. "I went to the library to look up our work and it was described by anthropologists as 'grotesque,' 'crude,' 'primitive,' and 'ugly.' It was just so offensive and that was when I became disenchanted as a student." Emmons himself described the piece as "a man whose face is in pain as if he had been hurt by a blow." Jonaitis describes the piece as a "horribly distorted visage, with its mouth and nose twisted painfully creating deep wrinkles on the right and taut stretched skin on the left." Emmons, despite his fascination with Tlingit material culture, neglected to document any information about the artist of the helmet, nor for the majority of the 4,000 pieces he collected while stationed in Sitka.

The *War Heads* drums, however, brought the helmet back to life when S'eiltin's brother and daughter used them during the Tlingit and Haida Celebration in Alaska in the summer of 2004. Also, "One of the drums was taken to a memorial potlatch and was recognized and honored as clan art, which is a great honor." For S'eiltin and her brother, who regularly travels and drums with them, these pieces "are not just for a museum or collections, they are living works of art."

While the drums are an affirmation of cultural heritage and an assertion of political repatriation, the artist also created them to intentionally shatter the romanticized stereotypes of peaceful nations with undefined territories.

I am interested in war regalia because it is an expression of resistance. Even though I don't approve of war I can see how important it is to tell stories of resistance, especially those that took place during contact. It's important for all to know that

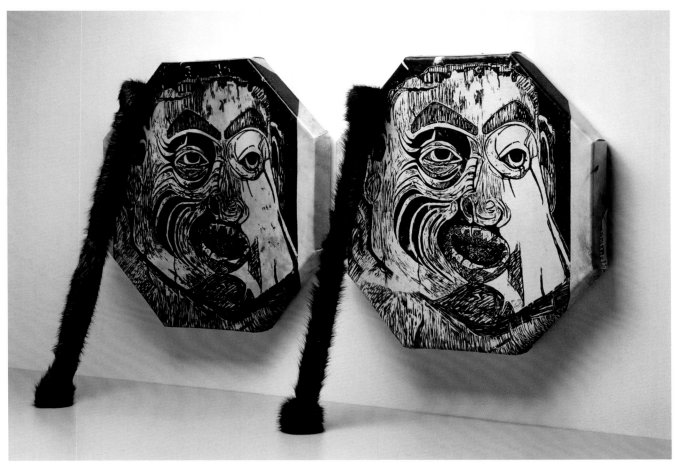

69. *War Heads*, 2003. Woodcut print on rawhide, wood, beaver, copper

we weren't passive by-standers or helpless victims, that we were active participants and aggressors, which is rarely taught in academia. Everyone respected hunting, fishing and trade territories, and we fought to protect those boundaries and maintain political boundaries.

Becoming a landless people is one of S'eiltin's concerns, which she has complexly intertwined in the large installation *Resisting Acts of Distillation,* 2002. Occupying 1,000 square feet, the installation challenges issues of individual land allocation, Alaskan corporate establishment and land stewardship, federal status recognition, and most dramatically, blood quantum requirements that have been integrated into all of these issues.

Flooded by an overwhelming ambience of redness is a huge curtain of

2000 vials, tied together in lines, each filled to the top with red wine. Behind the veil is a glowing red neon piece in the shape of a traditional copper, or *Tinnah.* Adjacent are fourteen shelves, each supporting a glass vase filled with water and a vial. Above the shelves are small rawhide prints, and below each are designations for the thirteen Alaskan Native Regional Corporations and one for S'eiltin's Village Corporation. The multiple dimensions of the installation resist separation and instead work together in political harmony to address the complexities surrounding the establishment and maintenance of the corporations.

S'eiltin initiates the dialogue from a long history of economic consumerism of Alaska's natural resources. First, the Russian fur traders who reached the

70. *Savage Apparel*, 2004. Bait box, baleen, beeswax, honeycomb paper, waxed thread, metal washers, fishing twine

71. *Savage Apparel*, 2004. Bait box, baleen, fish skin, honeycomb paper, metal, beeswax

73. *Savage Apparel*, 2004. Bait box, rawhide, copper wire, fish skin, bone, waxed thread

Aleutian Islands in the late 1700s, then the gold miners and fishers who came from the south, and finally the U.S. government in pursuit of domestic oil.[3] But before oil development could occur, land allocation had to be settled. According to Congressional reports, in 1971 Congress enacted the Alaska Native Claims Settlement Act (ANCSA) in order to "resolve Native aboriginal claims against the United States."[4]

Land settlement, however, is always made more complicated than need be, and ANCSA established approximately 200 Native Village Corporations for "surface estate of lands" with "subsurface estate to (13) Native Regional Corporations." The report continues, "Usually, the Regional Corporations could receive the lands beneath the Village Corporations in their area, but subsurface lands beneath pre-1971 refuges were not available, and in-lieu lands were substituted for them." Distinctions between surface and subsurface land enables wide governmental maneuvering in resource development, that is compounded by the limitations to exclusively recognize only village occupation in 1971—effectively denying and dismissing the 10,000-plus years of Native settlement throughout the region that was entered into U.S. statehood in January 1959. Furthermore, since having formed the Alaska Native Brotherhood and Alaska Native Sisterhood in 1912 and 1915 respectively, Native peoples have been working with imposing governments to address citizenship, equal rights, self-determination, education, Alaska Native civil rights, fishing rights, and land ownership.[5]

Each of the corporate designated shelves in *Resisting Acts of Distillation* supports a glass vase of water holding a vial filled with petroleum oil and corked with beeswax. The properties of the water and beeswax cork hold the petroleum oil vials perfectly upright in a delicate balance of innate nature. Behind the vases are block prints of an open hand on rawhide which "represent the loss of land as the majority of land is not individually or tribally owned, but corporate owned. The works question the transformation of identity standards of recognition."

With one-ninth of the state's land and $92.6 million dollars granted to the corporations, Native peoples have since acquired two identities—their corporate affiliation as well as their maternal clan and moiety.[6] "Tribal identity is now linked to corporate shares and commercial profits from the selling of natural resources. Former standards of tribal identity now translate to new standards of corporate wealth or poverty." An imposed corporate model invariably has limited potential for ensuring the personal welfare of its current stockholders and members, let alone the generations to follow. This form of economic genocide is inevitable when potential membership is governed by a specific cut-off date of birth. According to ANSCA, enrollment is based on rolls prepared by the Secretary "of all natives who were born on or before, and who are living on, December 18, 1971. Any decision of the Secretary regarding eligibility for enrollment shall be final."[7]

To possibly conceive that all individual native peoples could be or would be

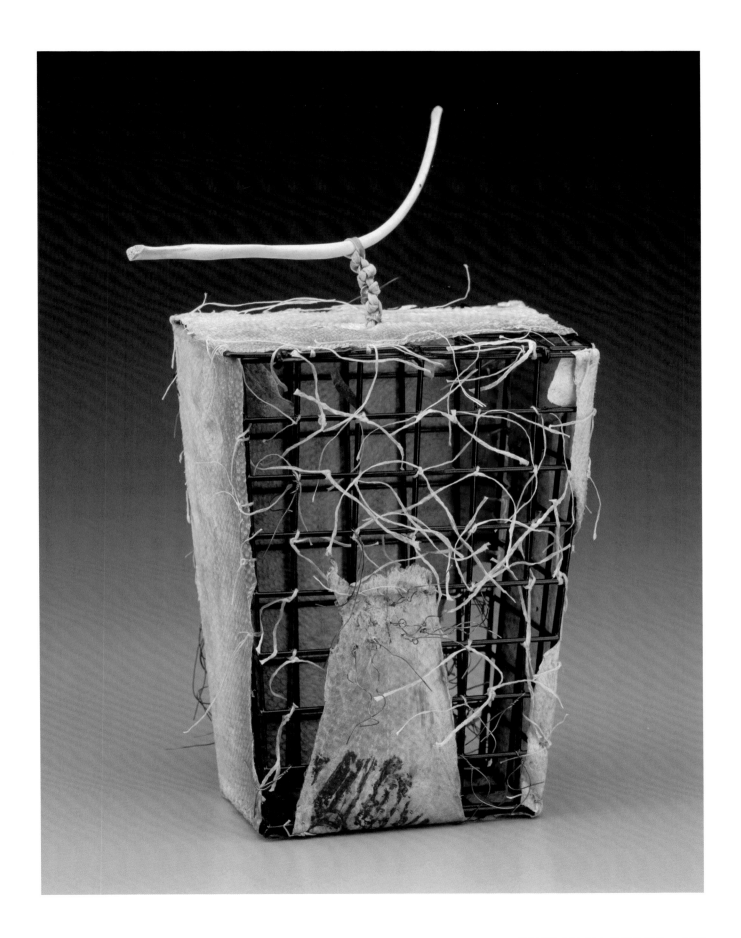

74. *Savage Apparel* (open), 2004
Bait box, honeycomb paper, beeswax,
beaver fur, smoked moosehide, bear
claw, metal, fish skin, waxed thread

listed on government lists and rolls is,
at best, foolhardy. Adoption, migration,
captivity, and governmental distrust are
only a few reasons why, historically,
Native Americans across the continent
have declined to acknowledge colonial
governments by signing their census
lists and rolls. Furthermore, to create
ANSCA, individual land claims also
had to be addressed. It was at this time,
in following the Dawes Allotment Act
of 1887, that Native people in Alaska
were assigned allotment numbers in
order to claim 160 acres, the great
majority of which have yet to be
granted. When such lists become linked

with economic advantages, then further
distinctions become invoked to deter-
mine one's eligibility.

The elaborate potlatch ceremonies,
the art created for them, and Native
languages document the strong oral histories of families and communities for
several generations on the Pacific coast.
Since 1971, however, the western
pseudo-measurement of blood quantum has become the imposed authority
for tribal and corporate membership.
The federal government issues official
Certificates of Degree of Indian or
Alaska Native Blood which "certifies
that an individual possesses a specific

degree of Indian blood of a federally recognized Indian tribe(s)."[8] Pure blood, ½, ¼, ⅛, ¹/₁₆ . . . living on reservations or in urban centers . . . federal relocation; it is difficult to keep track of the changing and variable standards for local and national enrollments.

The rich deep-red wine filling the vials evoking laboratory analysis brings the inequities of blood measurements from paper documentation to lifesize proportions. Representing individuals, the vials are tied together in lines to form the massive curtain. The installation is about strength, with each vial filled to the top "to represent that

despite all the things that have happened to us, and the corporations, that we still can identify ourselves."

The powerful neon *Tinnah,* also known as a copper, stands strong behind the vials reflecting the endurance of Native peoples. S'eiltin's invocation of the copper emerges from Coho clan history, since historically copper was distributed throughout the coast by the clan. The significance of the *Tinnah* is well documented throughout the entire coast. Its representation of wealth was very real, in the acquisition of the material itself and the symbolism it acquired through owner-

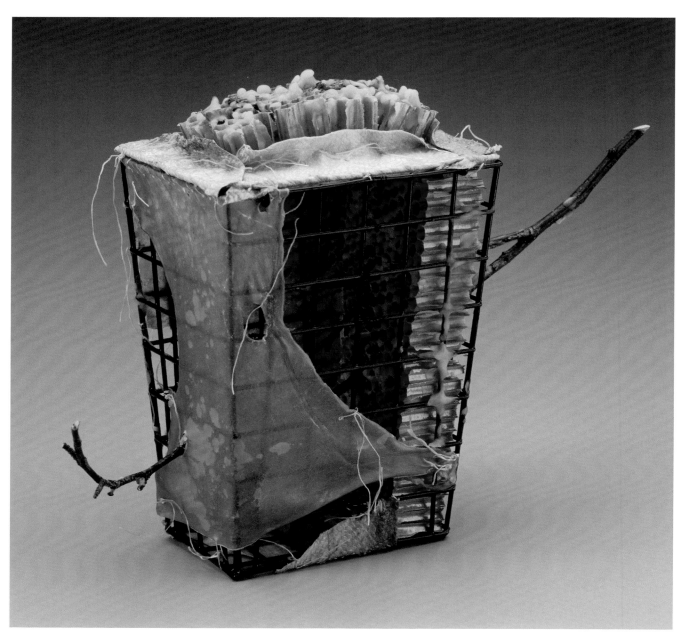

75. *Savage Apparel*, 2004. Bait box, rawhide, metal, copper wire, fish skin, beeswax, twig, waxed thread

ship, which was recognized yet further when the owner, in a demonstration of great wealth, would cut pieces off to give away at potlatch. S'eiltin brings this strength and prosperity to her installation, where the presence of the *Tinnah*, and thus her rich cultural heritage, is sustaining and enduring.

As if to guard the territory, people, and traditions, S'eiltin includes a large image of the Tlingit war helmet printed onto a large deer rawhide. The helmet

"represents our ability to resist entities that threaten self-awareness and cultural identity."[9] To resist distillation is to reject methods of separation, fueled by heat and volatile elements that foster the process, but S'eiltin brings all of these disparate elements together, maintaining and sharing her hopeful views of the future.

Looking to the next generation, S'eiltin completes both an ideological and matrilineal circle, when she recently collaborated with her daughter, Vanessa Omer, in the exhibition *The Naming* held at Skagit Valley College. "The exhibition was influenced by the naming process at potlatch and honored our matriarchal system. It honored my great grandmother, Mary Berries, from Yakutat." Together, they alluded to the clan house itself by creating a twenty-four by eighteen foot house of fabric. S'eiltin included neon and a large silk-screened image of her great-grandmother and great-grandfather, while Omer, in dramatic colors, painted names from both sides of her family history, commemorating her connection to her Tlingit grandmother and Tlingit women's names. Recognizing and continuing the matrilineal circle for the next generation, Omer states that her art "is my way of preserving and honoring the cultural traditions my mother and grandmother have taught me."[10]

NOTES

1. Unless otherwise noted, all quotations of the artist are from an interview with the author on August 12, 2005.

2. A. Jonaitis, *American Museum of Natural History: From the Land of the Totem Poles* (New York and Seattle: American Museum of Natural History in association with University of Washington Press, 1988), 110–112.

3. Artist Statement, Sacred Circle Gallery, Seattle, WA, May 3–23, 2005, www.ebuynativeart.com/Tanis/Tanis.htm

4. P. Baldwin, *Legal Issues Related to Proposed Drilling for Oil and Gas in the Arctic National Wildlife Refuge,* CRS Report for Congress (Washington, DC: Congressional Research Service, The Library of Congress, 2005).

5. B. Fleek, "Native Ways of Knowing: Experiences, Influences and Transitions of Tlingit Women Becoming Leaders" (master's thesis, University of Alaska, 2000). www.alaskool.org/projects/women/Fleek%20Thesis/NativeWays.html#background

6. Artist Statement on *Resisting Acts of Distillation,* The Eiteljorg Fellowship for Native American Fine Art, 2004.

7. Alaska Native Claims Settlement Act of 1971, Title 43, Chapter 33, Section 1604. www.ancsa.net/law/ancsa/1604>

8. Department of the Interior, Bureau of Indian Affairs, 25 CFR, Part 70, RIN 1076-AD98, Certificate of Degree of Indian or Alaska Native Blood. <http://cita.chattanooga.org/bia/cdibfedreg.htm

9. Artist Statement on *Resisting Acts of Distillation,* The Eiteljorg Fellowship for Native American Fine Art, 2004.

10. Vanessa Omer, Artist Statement. December cover artist, *Indian Gaming Magazine,* 2004. www.igmagazine.com/pages/437043/page437043.html?refresh=1107793878848

BACK TO THE BLANKET *Marie Watt and the Visual Language of Intercultural Encounter*

MARIE WATT *(Seneca)*

Many an Indian has accomplished his own personal salvation by "going back to the blanket."

—LUTHER STANDING BEAR[1]

Marie Watt's flags, samplers, columns, and other works made from reclaimed wool blankets evoke multiple referents in the history of art and the history of Native/white intercultural encounter. The trade blanket is, of course, a highly fraught item in cross-cultural exchange. Over the centuries, many meanings and divergent histories have been woven into its fabric. In her large-scale textiles and installations, Marie Watt unravels these multiple strands, offering a twenty-first century visual and emotional interpretation of a historic item.

Watt was born in 1967 to a Seneca mother and a Scots-German father, and grew up in Redmond, Washington, far from her mother's ancestral Seneca homeland, the Cattaraugus Reservation in New York State. After earning a Bachelor's degree from Willamette College in Salem, Oregon, she attended the famous program for Native students at the Institute of American Indian Arts in Santa Fe. Scholarships from the Seneca Nation, the Philip Morris Foundation, the American Indian Graduate Center, and the Kellogg Foundation financed her M.F.A. in painting and printmaking at Yale University from 1994–96. At IAIA, she discovered that she had something to contribute to the world of art-making. At Yale, she learned how important it was to her to make art focused on personal issues. Each educational experience was, in its own way, "both informing and deforming," Watt says. But the combination of IAIA and Yale prepared her for all aspects of the art market and the art world.[2]

Her current work filters all of these experiences, as well as her sense of the gravity of Native history, which she conveys through the weighty presence of wool blankets. To any viewer cognizant of Native art and history, Marie Watt's work evokes a 500-year saga of inter-cultural relations. This story pivots on the image of the blanket: an item that bespeaks not simply domesticity and warmth, but also the tangled histories of Natives and Europeans in North America.

In *Column,* 2003, the artist references blankets stacked for distribution by white traders as well as Native chiefs. The vertical tower of folded blankets also evokes totem poles, that quintessential Indian icon, and *Endless Column,* 1938, by the Romanian modernist Constantin Brancusi. Watt writes, "My approach to art making is shaped by the proto-feminism of Seneca (Iroquois) matrilineal custom, political work by Native artists in the 1960s, a discourse on multiculturalism, as well as quilts, beadwork, Mimimalism, Pop Art, and hard-edged abstraction."[3]

But it all starts with a modest, worn, domestic item, the blanket. As early as 1611 in New France (eastern Canada), Jesuits described Indians wearing wool trade blankets, some of them fashioned into *capotes*—loosely tailored overcoats. Throughout the next three centuries, blankets were central to economic exchange with Native peoples. Traded first for the highly prized beaver pelt so sought after in Europe for the manufacture of felted hats, blankets later were exchanged for many different skins and hides. French and English mills supplied the wool blankets. One 1851 chronicle from Fort Benton (in present-day Montana) describes fourteen types

76. *Column,* 2003. Installation

111

of blankets available for intercultural trade, while in Canada, Hudson's Bay Company archives chronicle 35,000 blankets being shipped to Victoria, British Columbia in 1864 alone, many destined for the great potlatches, or giveaway feasts of the Northwest Coast Indians.[4]

Native women had, in prior centuries, painstakingly made clothing out of animal hide, bark, and woven fibers. They immediately saw the possibilities inherent in trade blankets and other yard goods, and these became invaluable materials. Like artists everywhere, Native women embraced new media; wool blankets, glass beads, shell buttons, silk ribbons, and other materials from a global inventory of finery were put to new uses. They quickly learned to boil quills or plant fibers with bits of trade blankets to dye the natural materials scarlet or indigo. On the Northwest Coast, women used black and red English wool to make their distinctive button blankets, their crest patterns formed with mother-of-pearl buttons from the China trade. On the Great Plains, women fashioned wool dresses adorned with elk's teeth. In the communities of the Great Lakes and Southern Plains, Potawotami, Winnebago, Mesquakie, and other women adorned their trade blankets with imported silk ribbons in patterns that recalled their ancestral designs in plant fiber. Indeed, a multitude of artistic strategies were at play in the way indigenous women across the continent adapted trade woolens to their own artistic, ceremonial, and personal needs.

For many people, the term "trade blanket" conjures up a more modern rendition—that of the Pendleton blanket. The Pendleton Woolen Mills in Oregon commenced production of colorful jacquard-weave blankets in 1901. Their goods, along with those of several rival mills, were marketed across the United States.[5] Some designs were based on those of Native weavers, others on beadwork or basketry patterning. When Luther Standing Bear wrote in 1933 of "returning to the blanket," the Pendleton blanket is the image that would have arisen in the imaginations of his readers, Native and non-Native alike. For more than a century, Pendleton blankets have been part of a trade economy within Native nations, serving as gifts at powwows, giveaways, funerals, graduations, coming-of-age ceremonies, and other important rites of passage.

In addition to these histories of creativity, adaptation, and generosity, the trade blanket also brings to mind a more nightmarish history: the smallpox blanket. The deliberate infection of Native peoples with smallpox through the distribution of blankets taken from epidemic victims is a truism of American oral history. Though scholars can find little solid evidence that blankets were a deliberate vector of transmission, it is indisputable that millions of Native people died from smallpox, a European plague.[6] To this day, the story of the smallpox blanket is powerful, emblematic of half a millennium of injustices perpetrated upon Native peoples by those of European heritage. It is certainly an issue evoked in many viewers' minds when they see Watt's works.

As a twenty-first century artist exploring her hybrid legacies of Native

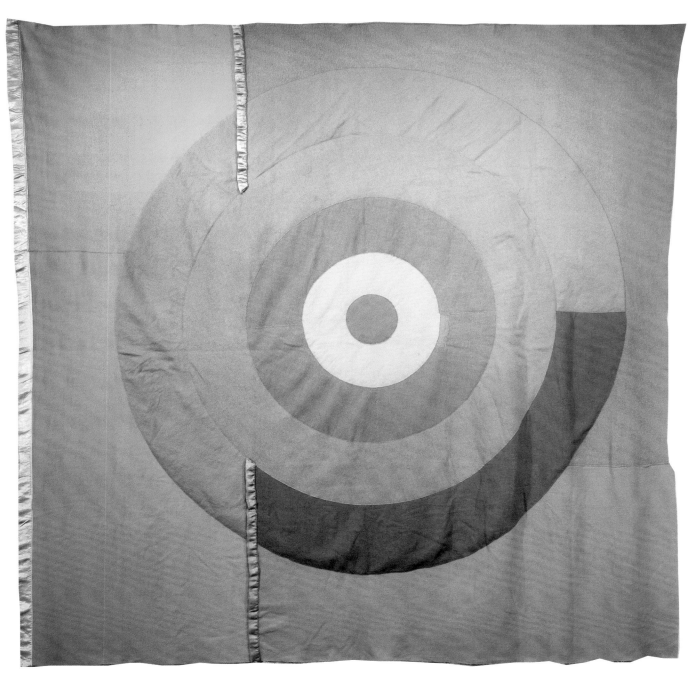

77. *Flag,* 2003. Wool, satin binding, thread

and post-modern art, Marie Watt has gone "back to the blanket" for inspiration, and for an iconographic language. She addresses complex visual and cultural histories with inventiveness, artistic rigor, and wit. Her work communicates the resourcefulness of women as well as the trauma of colonialism.

Trade blankets acquired by Native women in the historic period were finely woven products of European mills, or more recently, of American mills such as Pendleton. Watt turns this system of valuation on its head, for she scours secondhand and Goodwill stores for her worn and used blankets, items that have accrued multiple histories. Rather than calling these "found objects," as many contemporary artists might, Watt characterizes her material

78. *Color Study for Braid*, 2003. Reclaimed wool, satin binding, silk thread

as "*reclaimed* wool." This modifier suggests agency, activity; she is reclaiming the blankets and their meaning for a post-colonial Native American art, reclaiming the histories of ownership, and even the histories of sensation and emotion inherent in them.

The largest work exhibited here, the diptych *Braid*, 2004, is more than twenty-two feet across. Upon a gray wool background, the artist and her assistants have pieced a flattened Mobius strip composed of hundreds of diamond-shaped lozenges of fabric hand-sewn together. On the left side of the diptych, rivers of color flow from blue and green to yellow, orange, and red. This shifts into monochromy on the other side, where it also changes in scale. On the right side, the only color is the border pieced from the satin

blanket bindings that traditionally hemmed the top edge of wool blankets. A dozen rows of joined satin and wool blanket edges form the far border of the work. Of this piece, the artist has written:

Like the tradition of weaving hair, *Braid* is the weaving together of story, blankets, and sewers. I began with an interest in the many associations with braids: traditional native identity, a genetic marker, a ledger of passing time, and the intrusion of western educational reform (one of the first things stripped from native students in boarding schools was their long hair). Additionally, the braid's three skeins suggest various trilogies. In Seneca teachings, for example, we have the Three Sisters: Corn, Beans, and Squash. . . . While they are independent, the Three Sisters have more strength and vitality when they support each other. They rep-

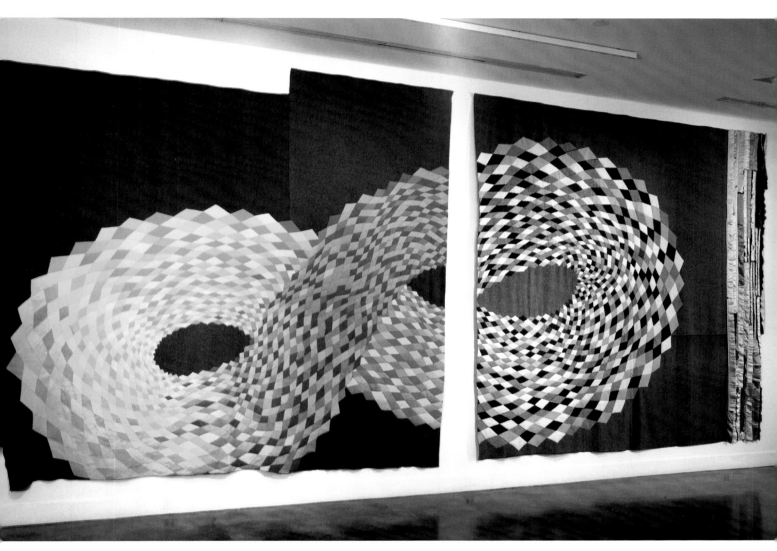

79. *Braid*, 2004. Reclaimed wool blankets, satin binding

resent the nutritional and spiritual sustenance of our community. *Braid* took on additional significance when friends and family came together for sewing bees to help complete the work. Watching my friends with their heads down, hands busy, stories flowing, I learned once again about the importance of community. My history is woven into these blankets, along with the wool, thread, and souls of 77 friends who sat around the pieces hand-stitching and story-telling, and transforming the blankets one more time.[7]

The pieced elements of *Braid* recall the star quilts composed of hundreds of diamond-shaped pieces that have been the favored pattern of Plains Indian quiltmakers for over a century.[8] The hand-cut and hand-pieced diamond shapes in *Braid* are neither precise nor mathematical in execution; instead they bespeak individual hands, producing different widths and tension in the stitches. So a work which, from a distance, may recall the hard-edged abstraction of Pop or Op art, on closer inspection reveals the domestic sensuality of the collective and the handmade.

Watt uses the same wool blankets to work in miniature scale, on pieces she terms "samplers." In *Color Study for Braid,* 2004, small squares of pink and dusty rose, gold and yellow, soft greens and blues rehearse the larger diamonds in *Braid,* as do the various grays and off-whites. In *Ladder,* 2004, the artist has interleaved several strips of worn, satin-bound blanket edges and sewn them to a wool backing. An irregular ladder of stitching on the right-hand side is the only ornamentation on these muted fragments of beige, sand, and teal.

Shift, 2004, is composed of fragments of blue blankets in which the satin binding has mostly been worn away except where it was stitched down. The artist has connected the pieces with simple stitches of rose-colored thread. The variation between the most worn areas (where one can see the warp and weft of the blankets), and those in which the fuzzy surface nap is most prominent, leads the viewer through a mediation on the humble poetics of wear and use.

Calling these "samplers," and framing them behind glass, recalls young women's work from eighteenth- and nineteenth-century America, when a girl's artistic education culminated in a finely wrought embroidered sampler of lettering and pictorial imagery.[9] Watt signs each with small stitched initials, MW, that are easy to miss, for they are subtle, and look almost like a blanket stitch. Watt's samplers are tiny abstractions as well as historical fragments.

Flag, 2003, which is roughly ten feet square, recalls historic American women's artistry on a larger scale: the quilt. While many Americans think nostalgically about the quilt as a polite and genteel art form, it was also, even in the nineteenth century, the place where women of an artistic bent worked out their ideas about color theory, abstraction, and geometry.[10] The graphic boldness of *Flag* also recalls 1960s Pop Art explorations of flags, targets, and banners, as does *Water/Sky,* 2005. The latter came out of an exploration of the many blue blankets the artist had collected. She was particularly intrigued with a blue-flecked Pendleton. Upon seeing the blanket, an artist colleague at the Oregon College of Arts and Crafts commented, "That looks like water-sky." And so the work was named.[11]

Watt sees her work as contributing to a larger dialogue about art, craft, and culture. She does not view herself primarily as a textile artist, for she has worked in diverse media, including paper, corn husk, stone, wool, bronze, and cedar. But about her blanket series, she says, "I'm going to be here for a while."

Her pieces in this exhibit provide continuity in, as well as transmutation of, historical women's arts, such as button blankets, ribbon skirts, samplers, and quilts. Moreover, her current work is part of an on-going visual conversation carried on by a number of artists, mostly Native and mostly female, who embrace the soft media used by their female ancestors.

Contemporary Navajo weaver D.Y. Begay's recent work *Two Points,* 2005, references trade blankets marked with black lines to indicate how many beaver

pelts they were worth.[12] Hopi weaver Ramona Sakiestewa has designed a series of blankets for production by Pendleton Mills. Mi'kmaq artist Teresa Marshall from Nova Scotia takes the black wool tradecloth that her great-grandmother's generation fashioned into tailored clothing and turns it into a garment both horrific and humorous. *Bering Strait Jackets #1 and 2* literally depict the way that Native peoples were figuratively straight-jacketed by treaties with whites.[13] Marianne Corless, an Anglo-Canadian artist, uses Hudson's Bay blankets to perform a visual critique of the sullied history of Native/white relations in her country. In *Blanket I,* 2002, the blanket is adorned with a red maple leaf, transforming the image into a Canadian flag. Smallpox pustules dot the surface of this virulent image.[14]

All these examples bespeak a renewed interest in fiber arts on the part of a number of younger women artists across North America. African-American artist Zenobia Bailey makes wearable art and fabric installations that draw from and comment upon the African and Afro-Caribbean heritage of women's crafts.[15] In her room-sized installation *Knitwork,* begun in 1992

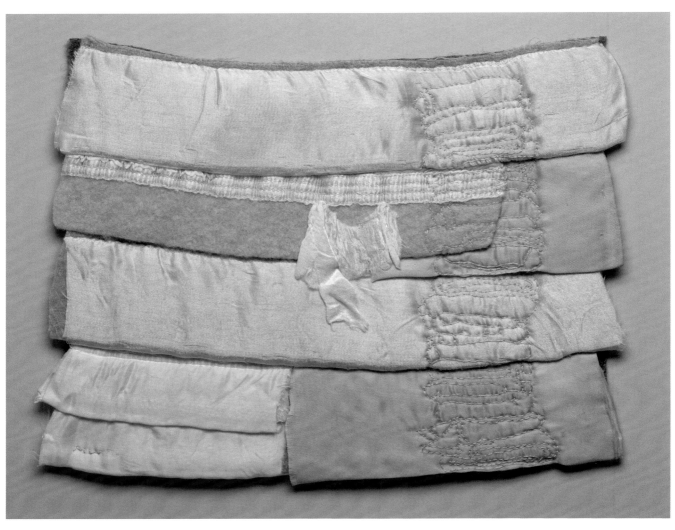

81. *Ladder,* 2004. Reclaimed wool, satin binding, silk thread

and ongoing, Malaysian-Canadian artist Germaine Koh unravels used garments and knits them into a multicolored piece strewn across a large gallery floor. She seeks to monumentalize the quotidian transactions of daily life in much the same way that Watt does.[16]

At a famous potlatch on Vancouver Island in 1895, one Kwakiutl chief boasted of his fame and stature, "the weight of my name is a mountain of blankets."[17] Indeed, photos of such potlatches show Hudson's Bay blankets stacked to the rafters in anticipation of their distribution as gifts by wealthy chiefs demonstrating their largesse. Examining the economies of power, art, and gender registered in Watt's work, we might revise the quote to read, in a more somber vein for our era, "the weight of our shared history is a mountain of blankets" (*Column,* 2003). In her poetic admixture of the elegance of modernist forms with the shabbiness of reclaimed materials, Marie Watt provides appropriate visual metaphors for our post-colonial and trans-cultural era.

NOTES

1. Luther Standing Bear, *Land of the Spotted Eagle* (Lincoln: University of Nebraska Press, 1978, original 1933), 7.

2. Personal communication from the artist, July 15, 2005.

3. Artist's Statement, Eiteljorg Fellowship Application, 2004.

4. For Fort Benton, see John Ewers, *The Blackfeet: Raiders on the Northwestern Plains* (Norman: University of Oklahoma Press, 1958), 69; for the Hudson's Bay Company, see W. R. Swagerty, "Indian Trade Blankets in the Pacific Northwest," *Columbia Magazine* 16 (2), 2002, 4. Between 1875–1899, more than 10,000 blankets were distributed at three Kwakiutl potlatches in British Columbia. These numbers rose even higher in the twentieth century. See Helen Codere, *Fighting With Property: A Study of Kwakiutl Potlatching and Warfare 1792–1930* (Seattle: University of Washington Press, 1950), 96.

5. See Charles Lohrmann, "Colorful Exchange: American Indian Trade Blankets," in *Chihuly's Pendletons* (Seattle: Portland Press, 2000), and Barry Friedman, *Chasing Rainbows: Collecting American Indian Trade and Camp Blankets* (Boston: Bulfinch Press, 2002).

6. The idea that there was a strategy of giving Indians blankets with the intention of infecting them rests on slim evidence: in 1763, one British colonel during the French and Indian War discussed in a letter "inoculating [i.e. infecting] the Indians by means of blankets." At Fort Pitt, that same summer, during Pontiac's siege of the fort, one militia leader wrote in his diary ". . .we gave them two Blankets and a Handkerchief out of the Small Pox hospital. I hope it will have the desired effect." See www.college.ucla.edu/webproject/micro12/web-pages/indianssmallpox.html for this documentation. A lively debate over this inflammatory issue can be found on the web.

7. Marie Watt, *Blanket Stories: Receiving* (Portland, OR: Hoffman Gallery, Lewis and Clark College, 2005), 9.

8. See Marsha MacDowell and C. Curt Dewhurst, *To Honor and Comfort: Native Quilting Traditions* (Santa Fe: Museum of New Mexico Press, 1997)

9. See, for example, Betty Ring, *Girlhood Embroidery* (New York: Alfred Knopf, 1993), 2 vols.

10. See, for example, Jonathan Holstein, *Abstract Design in American Quilts* (New York: The Whitney Museum, 1971); Janet Berlo and Patricia Crews, *Wild By Design: Two Hundred Years of Innovation and Artistry in American Quilts* (Seattle: University of Washington Press, 2003).

11. Personal communication from the artist, July 15, 2005.

12. This work, in the artist's own collection, is on display through 2005 in *Weaving is Life,* the Kennedy Museum of Art, University of Ohio, Athens.

13. *Bering Strait Jacket #1* is in the collection of the Eiteljorg Museum. See Colleen Cutschall, "Teresa Marshall: 'Wear the Media' is the Message," in W. Jackson Rushing, ed., *After the Storm: The Eiteljorg Fellowship for Native American Fine Art* (Seattle: University of Washington Press, 2001), 48–53, figs. 50, 51a and b.

14. See www.corless.ca (galblanket1.htm)

15. See Zenobia Bailey, *Mojo Medicine Hat,* 1999, and *Trilogy,* 2000, figures 11.1 and 11.2 in Lisa Farrington, *Creating their Own Image: the History of African-American Women Artists* (New York: Oxford University Press, 2005).

16. See Elissa Barnard, "Making the Mundane Remarkable," *The Halifax Herald Limited,* Sept 29, 2004. For other avant garde textile artists, see Ingrid Bachmann and Ruth Scheuing, eds., *Material Matters: The Art and Culture of Contemporary Textiles* (Toronto: YYZ Books, 1998).

17. See Franz Boas, *Kwakiutl Ethnography* (Chicago: University of Chicago Press, 1966), 89.

82. *Shift,* 2004. Reclaimed wool, satin binding, silk thread

83. *Water/Sky,* 2004. Reclaimed wool blankets, satin bindings

Contributors

JANET CATHERINE BERLO is Professor of Art History and Visual and Cultural Studies at the University of Rochester, New York. Her many books on indigenous arts of the Americas include *Spirit Beings and Sun Dancers: Black Hawk's Vision of the Lakota World* (New York: Braziller Press, 2001), *Native North American Art* (with Ruth Phillips, Oxford University Press 1998), and *Plains Indian Drawings 1865–1935: Pages from a Visual History* (Abrams, 1996). She also writes on nineteenth-century quilts and American visual culture (*Wild By Design,* University of Washington Press, 2003). Berlo has been a visiting professor at Yale and Harvard, and has received grants for her work on Native American art history from the Guggenheim Foundation and the Getty Trust.

JESSIE RYKER-CRAWFORD (White Earth Anishinabe) teaches both museum studies and indigenous studies at the Institute of American Indian Arts and Culture (IAIA) in Santa Fe, New Mexico. She graduated from IAIA with an AFA in both two-dimensional art and museum studies, and from the University of Washington with a B.A. in anthropology with a minor in Native American studies. She is currently a graduate student pursuing a Ph.D. in anthropology from the University of Washington with a focus on the politics of identity within contemporary Native American art. Her recent paper "The De-construction and Re-negotiation of Identity within Contemporary Native American Art" delves into the re-appro-priation of what it means to be "Indian" from Native artists throughout the country.

Ryker-Crawford has curated a number of exhibitions including the Quinault Tribal Center Exhibition, *In Commemoration of Beatrice "Grandma" Black: Quinault Basketry* and the IAIA Museum Exhibition, *The Fire and the Phoenix.*

JULIE DECKER has been a guest curator at the Anchorage Museum of History and Art for ten years. She is a co-director of the International Gallery of Contemporary Art and formerly owned the Decker/Morris Gallery, both in Anchorage, Alaska. She also works as an artist and a freelance writer. Decker has written numerous articles and publications on the art of Alaska, including *John Hoover: Art & Life, Icebreakers: Alaska's Most Innovative Artists* and *Found & Assembled in Alaska.*

VERONICA PASSALACQUA is a writer, curator, and researcher of North American Native art. She earned degrees at Harvard University and Oxford University and is currently completing her doctorate in museum ethnography from Oxford University. Passalacqua has recently been appointed junior specialist, women's studies, University of California at Irvine. Her curatorial efforts have included exhibitions at the Pitt Rivers Museum, Oxford, and the Barbican Art Gallery, London.

ALETA M. RINGLERO is an enrolled member of the Salt River Pima tribe of Arizona. An art historian and curator specializing in American Indian art history and criticism, she is the former director of Native American Public Programs, National Museum of Natural History, Smithsonian Institution. Currently, Ringlero is the founding curator of corporate collections for Casino Arizona at Salt River, and an art consultant to the architectural firm of FFKR, Architects, Salt Lake City, Utah. Ringlero recently graduated *magna cum laude* from Arizona State University with advanced degrees in Humanities and Art History.

W. JACKSON RUSHING III is Professor of Aesthetic Studies and Associate Dean of Graduate Studies in the School of Arts and Humanities at the University of Texas at Dallas. He has been a Fellow of the Guggenheim Foundation and the National Endowment for the Humanities. His major publications include *Allan Houser: An American Master* and, as editor, *After The Storm: The Eiteljorg Fellowship for Native American Fine Art, 2001*.

AMEI WALLACH is recognized as one of the most respected art critics in the United States. She is a frequent commentator on art for television and radio on both sides of the Atlantic. Educated at the University of Chicago, Columbia, and Stanford, Wallach has lectured and traveled widely, and reviewed every major exhibition in recent history.

Her books include the first monograph on *Ilya Kabakov: The Man Who Never Threw Anything Away* (Abrams, 1996) and *Reflections on Nature: Paintings by Joseph Raphael* (Abbeville, 1997). Wallach has contributed to numerous other books, including *Universal Limited Art Editions* (The Art Institute of Chicago, 1989), *Jasper Johns: Writings, Sketchbook, Notes, Interviews* (Museum of Modern Art, 1996), *Crossroads: Art and the Public Sphere* (New Press, 2001), and *Bruce Nauman* (Johns Hopkins Press, 2002).

Checklist

JOHN HOOVER *(Aleut)*
Distinguished Artist

1. *Adam and Eve,* 1960
   Oil on canvas, 16 x 20
   Courtesy of the artist

2. *Trollers,* 1964
   Oil on canvas, 24 x 20
   Courtesy of the artist

3. *Adam and Eve,* 1967
   Cedar, 42 x 21
   Courtesy of the artist
   (not illustrated)

4. *Aleut Ancestor Spirit Board,* 1970
   Cedar, 81 ½ x 12 ¼
   Courtesy of the artist

5. *Polar Bear Spirit,* 1971
   Cedar, 36 x 22 (open); 36 x 11 (closed)
   Courtesy of the artist

6. *Spirit Board,* 1973
   Cedar, 60 x 9 ¼
   Courtesy of the artist

7. *Sea Eagle Woman,* 1975
   Cedar, 108 x 56 x 13 ½
   Courtesy of the artist

8. *Seal People,* 1975
   Cedar, 44 x 22
   Collection of the Eiteljorg Museum

9. *Bird Woman (Dance Staff),* 1976
   Bronze, 95 x 23 ¾ x 19
   Courtesy of the artist

10. *Loon Man Soul Catcher,* 1980
    Cedar, 36 x 21 ½
    Courtesy of the artist

11. *Octopus Chimes,* 1981
    Bronze, 50 x 28 x 28
    Courtesy of the artist

12. *Underwater Loon Woman,* 1985
    Cedar, 46 x 11
    Courtesy of the artist
    (not illustrated)

13. *Winter Weasel Spirit,* 1985
    Cedar, 37 x 22 ½
    Courtesy of the artist

14. *Polar Bear Mobile,* 1987
    Cedar, 40 ½ x 23 ¾ x 23 ¾
    Courtesy of the artist

15. *Salmon Woman,* 1987
    Cedar and beads, 80 ½ x 38 x 18 ½
    Courtesy of the artist

16. *Hunting Scene, Self-Portrait,* 1988
    Cedar, 20 x 16 ½
    Courtesy of the artist

17. *Kushtaka,* 1988
    Cedar, 36 x 12 ½ x 12 ½
    Courtesy of the artist

18. *Seal Spirit Mask,* 1989
    Cedar, 21 x 11 x 2
    Courtesy of the artist

19. *And You Thought You Were Pregnant,*
    1992
    Cedar, 71 x 27 x 10 ¾
    Courtesy of the artist
    (not illustrated)

20. *Aleut Storyboard: Old Man of the Sea,*
    1993
    Cedar, 38 ½ x 73 ¼
    Collection of the Eiteljorg Museum
    (not illustrated)

21. *Baby,* 1993
Cedar, 23 ¾ x 20
Courtesy of the artist

22. *That's What You Get for Horsing
Around,* 1993
Cedar, 69 x 24 x 13 ½
Collection of the Eiteljorg Museum
(not pictured)

23. *Loon Lady,* 1994
Cedar, 35 x 30
Courtesy of the artist

24. *Blue Jay Man, Self-Portrait,* 1995
Cedar, 14 x 23
Courtesy of the artist

25. *Hummingbird Chimes,* ca. 1995
Bronze, 32 x 27 x 28
Collection of the Eiteljorg Museum
Gift: Courtesy of Martin J. and
Julie Klaper

26. *Great White Owl Spirit,* 1995
Cedar, 36 x 36 x 7
Courtesy of the artist
(not illustrated)

27. *Whale Rattle,* ca. 1995
Bronze, 13 x 4 x 2 ½
Collection of the Eiteljorg Museum
Gift: Courtesy of Martin J. and
Julie Klaper
(not illustrated)

28. *Loon People,* 1996
Cedar, 24 x 27
Courtesy of the artist

29. *Madonna and Child,* 1997
Cedar, 83 x 36 ½
Courtesy of the artist.
(not illustrated)

30. *Whale Family,* 1997
Cedar, 32 x 36 x 2
Courtesy of the artist

31. *Blue Footed Boobies,* 1998
Cedar, 24 x 27 ½
Collection of the Eiteljorg Museum

32. *Puffin Rattle (Female)* and
Puffin Rattle (Male), ca. 1998
Bronze
6 ¾ x 9 x 3; 6 ½ x 7 x 2 ½
Collection of the Eiteljorg Museum
Gift: Courtesy of Martin J. and
Julie Klaper
(not illustrated)

33. *Sun,* ca. 1998
Bronze, 36 ½ x 36 ½ x 6 ½
Courtesy of the artist

34. *Moon,* ca. 1998
Bronze, 36 ½ x 36 ½ x 6 ½
Courtesy of the artist

35. *Blue Jay Woman,* ca. 1999
Bronze, 38 x 9 ½ x 8 ½
Collection of the Eiteljorg Museum
Gift: Courtesy of Martin J. and
Julie Klaper

36. *Woman Shaman Transforming into Her
Eagle Spirit Helper,* 2000
Cedar, 64 x 27
Courtesy of the artist
(not illustrated)

37. *Bird Dancer,* ca. 2001
Cedar, 61 x 30 x 9 ½
Courtesy of the artist

38. *Bird Woman,* 2001
Cedar, 37 x 11 ½
Courtesy of the artist
(not illustrated)

39. *In the Beginning Raven Was White,*
2001
Cedar, 60 x 26 x 10 ¾
Courtesy of the artist

40. *Raven Stealing the Stars,* 2001
Cedar, 34 x 10 ½
Courtesy of the artist

41. *Salmon Women,* 2001
Cedar, 60 x 24
Courtesy of the artist
(not illustrated)

42. *Heron Soul Catcher,* 2003
Cedar, 54 ¼ x 28 x 10 ¾
Courtesy of the artist

43. *Copper River King, Copper River
Queen, Princess Loud Mouth,* 2004
Cedar, 54 x 50
Courtesy of the artist

44. *Mother Raven,* 2004
Cedar, 78 ½ x 13 ½
Courtesy of the artist
(not illustrated)

HARRY FONSECA
(Maidu/Nisenan, Portuguese, Hawaiian)

45. *Autumn Sonata #30,* 2002
Acrylic on canvas, 54 x 42
Courtesy of the artist

46. *Gold #2* (Mozart), 2002
Acrylic on canvas, 72 x 60
Collection of the Eiteljorg Museum

47. *Icarus #1,* 2002
Acrylic on canvas, 72 x 60
Courtesy of the artist

48. *Requiem #1,* 2002
Acrylic on canvas, 72 x 60
Courtesy of the artist

49. *Right of Spring #20* (diptych), 2003
Acrylic on canvas, 54 x 48
Courtesy of the artist

50. *Winter Solitude #9,* 2003
Acrylic on canvas, 30 x 24
Courtesy of the artist

51. *Red,* 2004
Acrylic on canvas, 20 x 20
Courtesy of the artist

Blue, 2004
Acrylic on canvas, 20 x 20
Courtesy of the artist

Black, 2004
Acrylic on canvas, 20 x 20
Courtesy of the artist

52. *For Annie: A Poem After Poe,* 2004
Acrylic on canvas, 36 x 48
Courtesy of the artist

53. *Illumination,* 2004
Acrylic on canvas, 48 x 36
Courtesy of the artist

JAMES LAVADOUR *(Walla Walla)*

54. *Bridge,* 2001
Oil on wood, 72 x 66
Courtesy of the artist

55. *Garden,* 2001
Oil on wood, 48 x 66
Courtesy of the artist

56. *Naming Tanager,* 2001
    Oil on wood, 72 x 96
    Courtesy of the artist

57. *Deep Moon,* 2004
    Oil on wood, 72 x 90
    Courtesy of the artist

C. MAXX STEVENS
*(Seminole/Muscogee Nations of the
Oklahoma Region)*

58. *Gatherers: Seven Sisters,* 2000
    Mixed media installation
    144 x 240 x 156
    Courtesy of the artist

59. *Book Ends: Al Is Between the Two
    Moons and on the Star,* 2004
    Book, mixed media
    8 ½ x 11 x ¼
    Courtesy of the artist

60. *Book Ends: As It Should Be,* 2004
    Book, mixed media
    7 ½ x 11 ¼ x 1
    Courtesy of the artist

61. *Book Ends: Centering,* 2004
    Book, mixed media
    8 ½ x 11 x ¼
    Courtesy of the artist

62. *Book Ends: Complexity,* 2004
    Book, mixed media
    8 ½ x 11 ½ x ¾
    Courtesy of the artist

63. *Book Ends: Memories of Childhood,*
    2004
    Book, mixed media
    9 ⅜ x 12 ½ x ¾
    Courtesy of the artist

64. *Book Ends: Process of Thought,* 2004
    Book, mixed media
    7 ¼ x 9 ½ x ½
    Courtesy of the artist

65. *Book Ends: Red Portrait,* 2004
    Book, mixed media
    7 ½ x 10 ¼ x ⅜
    Courtesy of the artist

66. *Book Ends: Shunatona Dance Steps*
    2004
    Book, mixed media
    8 ½ x 11 x ¼
    Courtesy of the artist

67. *Three Graces,* 2004
    Mixed media installation
    300 sq. ft.
    Collection of the Eiteljorg Museum

TANIS MARIA S'EILTIN *(Tlingit)*

68. *Resisting Acts of Distillation,* 2002
    Mixed media installation, 700 sq. ft.
    Courtesy of the artist

69. *War Heads,* 2003
    Woodcut print on rawhide, wood,
    beaver, copper, 30 (diameter)
    Collection of the Eiteljorg Museum

70. *Savage Apparel,* 2004
    Bait box, baleen, beeswax, honeycomb
    paper, waxed thread, metal washers,
    fishing twine, 28 ½ x 9 x 3 ¼
    Collection of the Eiteljorg Museum

71. *Savage Apparel,* 2004
    Bait box, baleen, fish skin, honeycomb
    paper, metal, beeswax, 36 x 6 ½ x 3 ¼
    Collection of the Eiteljorg Museum

72. *Savage Apparel,* 2004
Bait box, rawhide, fish skin, railroad
spikes, metal, fluorescent light,
10 x 8 x 4
Collection of the Eiteljorg Museum
(not illustrated)

73. *Savage Apparel,* 2004
Bait box, rawhide, copper wire, fish
skin, bone, waxed thread, 11 x 6 x 4
Collection of the Eiteljorg Museum

74. *Savage Apparel,* 2004
Bait box, honeycomb paper, beeswax,
beaver fur, smoked moosehide, bear
claw, metal, fish skin, waxed thread,
10 x 8 x 8 ½ (closed),
12 x 10 x 8 ½ (open)
Collection of the Eiteljorg Museum

75. *Savage Apparel,* 2004
Bait box, rawhide, metal, copper wire,
fish skin, beeswax, twig, waxed thread,
9 ½ x 13 ½ x 4 ½
Collection of the Eiteljorg Museum

MARIE K. WATT *(Seneca)*

76. *Column,* 2003
Installation, 22 x 26 x 96
Courtesy of the artist

77. *Flag,* 2003
Wool, satin binding, thread, 126 x 132
Courtesy of the artist

78. *Color Study for Braid,* 2003
Reclaimed wool, satin binding,
silk thread, 8 x 15
Courtesy of the artist

79. *Braid,* 2004
Reclaimed wool blankets, satin
binding, 128 x 259
Collection of the Eiteljorg Museum

80. *Found,* 2004
Reclaimed wool, satin binding,
silk thread, 6 ¼ x 6 ½
Courtesy of the artist

81. *Ladder,* 2004
Reclaimed wool, satin binding,
silk thread, 10 x 13 ½
Courtesy of the artist

82. *Shift,* 2004
Reclaimed wool, satin binding,
silk thread, 9 ⅞ x 8
Courtesy of the artist

83. *Water/Sky,* 2004
Reclaimed wool blankets, satin
bindings, 115 x 126
Courtesy of the artist